DESTROY ME,
DESECRATE MY
BONES

a collection of longings

Editing: Kelsey Sipple
Cover design: Matthew Barkley
Cover art: Harry Clarke for Edgar Allan Poe's *The Mystery of Marie Rogêt*

ISBN 979-8991853026 (paperback)
ISBN 979-8991853033 (ebook)

First Edition
Published by Girl Noise Press
girlnoise.press

"i just want some recognition for having good tits and a big heart"

— Reneé Rapp

For the longing heart of my sister Emma.

For the growing heart of my niece Karleigh.

DESTROY ME, *DESECRATE MY* BONES

a collection of longings

Victoria Hood

A Collection of Longings:

I. How many skeletons are in your closet? Are they yours? Are they friends? Have your ghosts hit puberty yet; are they thirsty? Adrenaline seekers? Do they wish to feel the sea spray in their face at high speeds? Do you want to go out for coffee after this?

II. Where is your scientist? Who's the fraud? Have you applied? It's time to be examined. Are you ready?

III. Do you want to drip? To disappear? To be gathered, then unspooled? Are you married? Does it matter?

IV. Do you know where the bogs are? All of them? Are you made of molding clay? Are you in danger? Is that blood? Do you like that?

V. Are you collecting your loves? Do they keep spilling over? Do you want them all anyway?

VI. Will you cut and re-sew things to make them fit? Is this a ritual? Have we reached the bottom yet?

To Contain

THE HOUSE

The House knows Morse code.
It is telling me that it longs for me.
I am aching to understand if it is real.
I want to whisper to it that I feel its warmth.
I am aching to stay inside of it forever.

I am aching
I am aching

I know that these words are for me, I live alone, I am unattended
in a home that is in love for me, in a home that is my protector,
in a home that is learning how to speak to me [and to those
outside it speaks for me].

Do not let them in
Do not let them in

When the rain gets too heavy The House aches with water.
The House tells me that the roof has become such a burden.
The House warns me of the places where there should be
buckets.

I am wanting
I am wanting

The House learned Morse code for me, specifically.
I have never felt as special as when I realized it was me it always
wanted.
There was a time in which my mother told me the house I made
was ugly and disgusting and contained too many empty cans and
dirty dishes.
I now know that I understand The House more than she did.

I am aching
I am aching

I am aching.
I am aching.

CLOSET

You go back in the closet every night. You sleep under a fabric cloud. You rest your eyes and think of the ways in which this closet is easier, the ways in which a slow suffocation is easier than a yell and a show. When you fall asleep you only dream of the ways in which this closet could hold your whole world if you had enough hangers — the velvet ones, never the plastic — you crave softness (both for yourself and others).

Outside of your closet is a world without softness, a world without your comforter. No pillows to lay on, no sheets plastered with your own future and cum. Inside of your closet is a bed and your phone, the used water bottles that never seem to make it out, your favorite socks and all of your undies. Inside of your closet is a piece of comfort you keep hidden under your pillow, in between the mattresses, like the Princess and the Pea. Inside your closet you are a princess and you can wear your crown, you can do whatever you want, you make the rules.

The harsh brightness of the sun never seems to leak its way into your closet. If you could hide in there forever, then finally you'd be a vampire, you could lure the hot young people in just by batting your eyes, we know that it works.

But how would you afford your closet if you never leave? Vampires can't survive in a capitalist society, they are sucking the wrong thing. So you leave your closet when the day breaks through the clouds. You muster your pants and shirt into a matching set and you reset your eyes from drop dead gorgeous to just plain old beautiful — we don't need to repeat the incident from last time. You moisturize and deodorize and spray your cologne that is trapped inside our noses. You put on your human suit but laying under the surface is the sucker you always are. Out in the daytime you glisten when you smile, that is why you try to keep it hidden, you don't want your secret out (not everyone needs to know): you have a closet at home filled with bodies and bodies and old bodies that you've molted out of. During the day you act like this is the only body you've ever known, the only body you will ever know, during the day you act like this is *your* body.

But at night you lay naked with your tendons revealed, your eyes unset, uneasy, just waiting. At night you lay in your closet and wish there was a place for sex-addicted vampires that you didn't need to hide. That someone would open their veins to you and shower you in their juices. At night you think about the times when being you was okay and you hide in the corner of your closet even though you know no one is looking for you. You have the only key. You hide in your corner, scared of the dark.

Making the Move

I move in on the weekends. Our weekends, anyway. I move in on a Monday, and on Wednesday morning, I pack my things into my bags and you drive me away. I do not leave anything behind, I take all of my items: my stowaway toothbrush, my refillable deodorant, the strings I pull from your socks, all the candy words you give me on strings. On Wednesday morning, you drive me away and ask me to hop out while you test something. I wait there for my next ride.

Some weeks I come back early. I pack a duffel bag with well wishes that I sling over my shoulder. You meet me out back of my work and I stuff myself into an envelope you can slip into your pocket. You take me home and unfold me, you let me breathe out the wrinkles and fog. On these nights I lay next to you, rarely any time for anything else; on these nights I rest my head on your chest waiting to hear if your cyst will rupture; on these nights I feel so honored that you want to curl up next to me that I do not sleep; I just watch you rest; on these nights, I don't even bother unpacking.

Some weeks I fade into the forest until you can stand to see more of me. I pretend to be a tree that you can chop down when you are ready (precut). I know your mind is too full of tools you never get to use: the axe, the paring knife, the spoon you grind when you're anxious. You can cut me with anything you want, you can chew me until I fall over.

On the weekends, I unpack my bag at your place: in the corner, I leave my pile of clothes (never the right options), on your coffee table, I stack my jewelry in a pile, the branches and twigs that are caked in my hair, the lingerie that hasn't been bleached by my pussy, the cock ring we broke the first time we used it. On the weekends, I unpack myself: I tell you how I really feel, how scared I am of the forest, the thoughts that creep in with the bugs at night, the sounds that scare me, the list of longings that I'll never stop writing. On Wednesday, I pack this all up: with your leaking brain, with your sharp fingernails, with the jokes you won't stop telling. On Wednesday, I pack you back into my heart like a folded envelope and I keep you close.

The only thing left: the lighter I leave so I'll have something to smoke.

HOPELESS

I didn't know I was in an abusive relationship until years later. I didn't know you were abusing me until I told our quirky stories and the room filled with silence. Until my new best friend said, that was abuse. Until I actually stopped to consider the way you tried to undress me in public, the way you told me how to act, who to act with, until I stopped being so in love with you. Until I actually lost you, I didn't realize I needed to.

I wanted so much to fill myself with the things you liked. To drown myself with the hope of being enough for you, but there is no way to please changing standards; you always dust moving and moving and moving upward.

Selective Solitude

I always found you hiding under staircases you shouldn't be under. It seemed to me, then, that you didn't know what you were doing. I know now that you just loved the privacy. I often find myself thinking about how you fit under all those stairs, those vertical walls climbing the buildings. You never looked trapped, only lost in thought. I wished I could have joined you, but you never left enough space for me.

I always found myself wondering what you thought of me. A girl outside of staircases, always seeming to lurk for you. I thought of myself as endearing, as allowing space for us, as a friend of yours that you needed to get to know better. I never found myself thinking of the ways in which you might find it creepy — me always on the stairs you were under, not a gatekeeper but a follower to gates.

I admire the way in which you let me latch onto you — a lost and lonely girl trying to attempt a life worth living. I admire that you let me live yours. There were moments of wonder when we would take flight into a night that did not know we were coming. Running around cities that did not let us love them. Hand in hand as we found reasons to slip into alleys for hugs and kisses, scared of the eyes of the street. I admire the way in which you showed me off in solitude without me realizing, hiding me under your own gaze.

You told me then that this time would be different. That I was not another girl that sat on the stairs, I was more than that. I was the girl you wanted sitting on the stairs waiting for you. I realize now this must have been true. I think it was the way in which I was patient. I would miss class for you. I would run away if you needed. Though I was not a murderer, I could have been for you — another member of the cult you didn't know you were forming.

I think there must have been a moment when I realized the truth that stairs are an obstacle and truly not that friendly; that only spiders and creeps hide in the crevices, too scared of daylight to come out — to emerge. There must have been a day when I realized your nighttime ways and the softness of your palm covering my face and we breathe each other in. I think this moment must have lived just beneath the surface of my brain — too foggy to read.

I remember the way in which it felt to find your friends hiding there with you. The space seemed so immense then, like a whole city that lived just below me. You with the people you actually loved, dwelling in the town that I sat on top, of thinking I was some sort of ruler, thinking I had some sort of say. You loving the solitude as a way to hide the way you loved someone else.

First Impressions

The first thing I noticed about you was your teeth.

    The way they looked like glue.

        The way they seemed to be stapled into your mouth,

        they would never come out, the way they glowed

        in the dark of my brain, the first thing I wanted to do

        was taste them.

                To lick them clean.

The second thing I noticed was the size of your hands.

    The way they seemed to smile at me.

        I pictured them inside of me and wondered if

        your hand would fit,

        if you could wear me like a glove or

if perhaps I was too small to fit on top of you.

I've wondered about you every time I see a piece of my house missing. When I see bite marks in the ceiling and the floors, I know you have been thinking of me too. When I walk down the street and notice all the people who seem to have their teeth missing I know that you have visited them.

You're like a tooth fairy but permanent

you only collect adult teeth.

THE MARRIAGE

I'd rather fuck a spider than get married. I would let it burrow inside of me and make a nest, it could lay its babies inside of me, a home for my homemaker. If I got married there would be nothing to do but knit a web to remind me of the spider, of the home it promised me. I felt like I had always been honest with you about this before, so I wasn't sure now why I was in the situation with you on one knee and people cheering, expecting the answer to be yes. It was not something to make me seem like a contrarian, it wasn't really even political. Truly, it was the need and knowledge that I own myself. That I do not belong to you.

I sold off parts of myself many times years ago. My heart a crumbled organ, no longer worth donating. I had even given my liver to the guy that was in that band that I really truly thought was going to make it. My brain always wanting to be too smart, too good for all those people crumbling at my feet. I wanted to tell myself I knew better, but the truth is that better is something that you cannot know.

I thought back to the time that I met you in the weirdly uncrowded bar. Your friend drunkenly hitting on my friend, you drunkenly hitting on me. We bonded over the deaths of our parents, wounds we no longer needed to lick. I told you I was an existentialist, you told me you were a nihilist and I think we both fell in love right then. It was the first and only time I ever danced until my legs fatigued, I collapsed into your arms, in your mouth, I thought you were going to eat me right there on the uncrowded dance floor — my friend now with a couple looking for a third and your friend really not getting the hint.

I looked at you now, kneeling below me and something about this made me kind of wet. The power of "no" finally came to mind. The way in which I could publicly humiliate you and walk away, I could find that spider and finally have a home. "Yes," I said. Reciting the lines I knew you wanted. The crowd seemed then like they knew everything they needed to know about our relationship. They knew we were in love enough to display it for them. They didn't know that I walked out on you later that night.

Application for Cohabitation Form P-M-94X

"The thing I don't think you're understanding is that we are not both registered poets. That's what I've been trying to explain to you and the five other people we had to talk to. He is a musician, a lyricist, a man of woodwinds and wind chimes and all the sparkly music makers. I'm the only poet, the only pencil-and-paper girl in the house."

"We understand your frustration but the law is very clear that only one poet can live in a house at a time. Unfortunately, your partner's file was flagged because his music is too closely related to poetry. What this means is that we cannot allow a poet of your degree to live with a musician of his manner. We hope you understand."

"Of course I don't understand! There is a huge difference between my poetry and his *music*. He writes *punk* songs for goodness sake — what kind of poetry is written about puking on people and grocery stores. I'll tell you what kind — not the kind you can get state-registered."

"We hear you, we really do. Unfortunately, this is something that is just out of our hands."

"Maybe I can clear this up, being the musician and all. There is *no* cross-boundary work going on here. The only reason we want to live together is because we love each other and it comes with double the amount of groceries and rent that we currently have. Is there any way to unflag my file? Maybe if I played a bit for you then you'd understand there was nothing to be worried about?"

"You can put your guitar away, sir. Did you write, *'And all that bleeds out of me are tiny bits of you / Always protruding and stabbing, always my memories of you'*?"

"When I was much younger, yes, but — "

"If you are the one who wrote that then I cannot simply unflag your file. Did you also write, *'In my dreams I frame your body in blue paint, I fill in the words with my tongue'*?"

"Well yes but we were just messing around, that isn't what I normally — "

"You submitted it to your government file, didn't you?"

"I just thought it might get picked up and sold, I didn't want to publish it with my band."

"Unfortunately for you, that is something we cannot over-look. It is important that we restrict multiple poets from living in the same house. Have you heard of June of 2031? Or have they simply stopped educating the *punks*?"

"No, I've heard of it. I understand that in the group mentality there is a chance for poets to have an increased suicide rate but what we're discussing is completely different."

"Completely different than a poet converting a musician to start a death cult. Yes, I suppose *your* situation is far less original than you think. What I can offer you is the opportunity to convert your partner to a musician in which case you would have no trouble registering to live together. As you likely know, musicians have a cap of eight per household — fifteen if you're registered as a ska band."

"That is where I have to draw the line. Do you know how hard it is to become a registered poet? I spent two additional years alone in a grad school just to see the registered **P** next to my name. I'm not just going to simply re-register."

"Which is exactly what you told us the last three times we offered you this option. It seems today like we won't be coming to an agreement."

"Wait! Wait! What if I registered the least poetic song right now? Can the flag be erased through clear evidence that poetry is not in my interest?"

"Please sir, I ask you again to put away your guitar. Even if that were an option, we would only need a lyric sheet. We never, and I emphasize, *never*, require the song to be played to be registered."

"Well here are some lines: *Piss on my face while I eat your shit / I want to drown in your blood / I want to crawl in your slit / We are bringing the flood.*"

"Though this would count as low-tier musical quality, which lines up perfectly with your punk music registration, I'm afraid it will not override the poet flag. However, you can wait the required one month until the flag disappears *given* you do not register any poetic lyrics during this time."

"Fine. We'll see you in a month."

I'm Sorry We're Getting Married

I love you, Harry. And of course I would marry you again, but maybe we should have waited. We could have waited until people did not ask if we meant it, if we thought it through. We could have waited until we had the courage to get what we wanted — or the money to feel like we could have an opinion. I love you, Harry. But maybe we should have waited until thirty. That seems to be when people say it is okay.

I wonder how much of this is personal anxiety, my constant fear of commitment that I combat with non-monogamy. I know some of it though, is the whispers of our friends who seem to smirk at the idea that five years was long enough, or twenty-four was old enough. I wonder how you're feeling, you always seem so sure. It's not that I wonder about you but that I wonder about age and if it matters.

I love you, Harry. And I'm excited that we can be married for most of our lives. What does that mean, though, when we can already love each other for most of our lives whether the government is involved or not.

I love you, Harry. But now I am thinking that we could have made a statement, a political social commentary of the institution of marriage by refusing to succumb. I love you, Harry. And I'm wondering what, if any, amount of rebellion is on our shoulders. Are we supposed to decline the expected to make a point? Who will do it if we don't? But the truth is that I love you, Harry. And I want to be the one to decide when to pull the plug in the hospital because I know you better than anyone and we talk about it all the time.

I wonder why sometimes I bothered to want to get married if I knew that I would never stop wanting to have sex with strangers. It's not just me. There are other relationships, other people, other marriages that opt for a sense of openness, a shirk at the concept that you should have one dick or one cunt forever. I love you, Harry. Because you too, are one of those people.

I love you, Harry. And now I'm thinking that we could have waited until I knew if I was done going back and back and back to school. But then there is the question of insurance in a country that doesn't care if you live unless you've decided to marry someone who can help you. I love you, Harry. And I'm wondering if it's insurance fraud to marry even if you don't believe in the institution of marriage. But you are a bartender and someone needs to bring home the healthcare.

I love you, Harry. And I wonder if we would have called it off by now if your parents were not religious or if they hadn't put so much money in. We've talked about it before how our wedding is not the one we are having but that it is okay because we are the spouses we wanted.

I love you, Harry. But we're not even sure if we want kids anymore. Wasn't that the first reason we gave? If we want kids we might as well make it easier and get married. But now we never seem to agree, when I want kids you don't, when you want kids I don't. I think about the disappointment it would be, to our families, your parents.

I love you, Harry. But maybe we're doing ourselves a favor. If we don't have kids then we don't have to disappoint your parents even more with the fact that they won't take your last name, or mine. Rather we want to combine combine combine. I love you, Harry. But I'm nervous that once we told your parents we wouldn't baptize our children they will look for a daughter-in-law elsewhere. I am nervous they would scoop you up and take you out out out of my life. I love you, Harry. But I've always had control issues and you can't control a child, not in the way that I want to control control. A child is a person and not an extension of me, they are an individual and individuals scare me.

I love you, Harry. But I think I've answered my question. Maybe I answered yours as well. Either way, however we think, I will see you at the wedding in July.

A Home Somebody Used to Know

They were inviting for people who would let you do anything that fit into the rules they had. Both named and unnamed. There was an expectation for knowledge that you may have lost in the mail, or maybe they never sent it. They were inviting for people who wanted to be thought of as inviting. And so they created a home that was inviting under certain circumstances.

———

And a girl fell in love with a boy who was birthed by these parents (or so they say — there is still a conspiracy theory of his adoption that is prolonged by the girl he loves and other people who love the girl). This girl was happy to be in a family as normal as the boy's, because in his family, people didn't kill themselves. Instead, they waited to die until it was the right time to do so, until the world said so — and I guess God, because the boy's parents were the kind of people who still believed in God even though they were well-educated (a paradox the girl never understood and often felt reduced the perceived knowledge of the parents of the boy she loved and sometimes even of the boy she loved because he believed too but differently and better).

The girl in this story was young and happy and even content, which was a word she never understood. The boy in this story was just as young and happy and even content, which neither of them understood. The girl and the boy in this story were happy and content even though there was a war inside themselves, but now they had created an army. Together, they felt like they could take on the thoughts that seemed to eat and creep and breathe and bite. Together, they had an army that felt like it could win both the offense and the defense, like they could barricade themselves inside their house and finally be happy and even content together.

On the inside, this army was the both of them and it would fight and fight the things that never asked to live inside of them but did anyway. On the outside when they were in the home of his parents the army was dismantled and the boy forgot to give the girl the instructions to the house that he had grown up in. The girl felt like she was set up to fail. The girl felt like an intruder to the other side. The girl felt like the boy she loved was lost somewhere in the war, like he had switched sides and joined the house of the rules, the house with the manual, the house of intruders. The army was reduced to a lonely girl in a house without the proper manual.

The girl often confronted the boy about how he turned from her boy to a thing like a lamp in the corner with a broken bulb that felt like an object she had never known. The girl felt like her boy was less of her boy and more of a stranger that forgot how to laugh or smile and now she understood why he couldn't have understood happy or content before. The girl watched as the boy entered the house with love on his lips and the longer he stayed the longer his lips seemed to fade, seemed to disappear, seemed to become swallowed in the rules and expectations of the house. The girl would ask the boy why he felt so different in the house, why his velvet skin became wet and matted, but all the boy could say was things were easier this way.

———

That was the thing the girl never understood, but she tried really hard to. She read passages about the way people deal with families who feel more like strangers. She tried to watch and analyze the way in which the words fell out of his mouth in different shapes and sizes in this house rather than in their own home. Most importantly, the girl thought about the way in which she could reshape herself to fit this home, to fit the boy that shifted and changed, camouflaging himself in the house with the wallpaper.

———

The boy felt sorry for the way in which he would harden into inanimate objects around the people who gave him life. He had respect for the life that was thrust upon him, and an understanding that it was expected for him to enjoy this life. He was sorry for the war that was rushing through him and so often when he went back to his house, the war would get worse and worse, but when he was in this home, the army was not together but disbanded and he wasn't sure how to fight on his own after having the support of their army. At night, sometimes they would hold each other, and the boy would whisper sweet things in her ear like he would in their own home miles away, but when the morning came and they went downstairs it was always the same — the boy became a lamp with a broken bulb and the girl watched him break.

———

The girl and the boy stayed in love but in a place that was far away from the house with the rules. They created and crafted and curated a home with less and less and less rules that let the army join forces and at night they would hide in their bunker and cuddle so closely the enemies thought they were one. The girl and the boy ran away, but close enough to sometimes have to return and slowly the girl understood some of the rules, but also, the girl hated the rules. The boy had a respect for sorts of authority like the kind he had been raised in, but the girl was raised differently. The girl was told that authority is negotiable and what is authority anyway and really the only authority we have is over ourselves and to remember that. So she could be stubborn in her ways of dismantling rules and reconstructing her own authority. So she did some things the wrong way, because she was tired of being a lost girl. The girl had always hated shoes and that included slippers, so she would wear her feet or socks around their floors and every time they asked why she was barefoot, she said it was because she liked it. And the boy understood even though he did not like it.

———

But the problem is that the girl was not alone. She had siblings who were even more stubborn to dismantle than her. In this story, the girl had a family all along, just not one with a house with rules. They used to have an apartment like a commune, but eventually that ended up losing its funding when their father left and their mother died. In this story, the girl was close to her siblings all along, but they all had their own path and their own rules in their own homes. In this story, the siblings had homes that felt like a warm blanket out of the dryer, but their homes were too full for two people in love.

———

That was, except for the sister who was really more like the best friend, who was really more like the daughter the girl felt she sometimes had. So now the girl and the boy and the girl's sister stayed at the house with rules, which meant that more people had to learn more rules and those rules started to become less and less printed and more and more memorized. The thing is that the sister never had a great memory and honestly, the girl wasn't a great teacher and soon it became less about slippers and more about the language and content of the girl and her family.

———

But the boy and the girl got married anyway, and now they sit at night and think about the ways in which if they have kids, the kids will have grandparents with a house with rules and the boy and the girl do not want the kids to have these rules and so it is a struggle of wondering if the kids can understand what it means to break rules in the right ways.

———

And so when they got pregnant, they aborted the baby because they still didn't understand the rules or how to teach them. Instead, they were waiting for the house with the rules to die, to become nothing but a house that people once loved.

To Devour

I'VE FALLEN IN LIKE

I've fallen in like and I can't get up. In fact, I'm not even trying. The further I try to pull my body, the bigger the hole that eats me gets. I am consumed with the curves of your teeth, the way I can fall inside your mouth when you open it to laugh, the way I am transfixed by the glow of your smile. My knees are buckling at the sound of your voice, my knees break apart and tumble when you say my name, I have fallen to the pavement, in like, and I can't get up.

I've broken my nails falling head over heels. Actually, I fractured my wrist. I tripped over your perfect body, laying sleeping, eyes resting like you were practicing for a nap. I saw the way your hair lays across your face and I couldn't help but leave my eyes behind with you. I tripped, I couldn't see, and I've broken my nails falling head over heels. I tried to catch myself, but all I could do was fall further and further again and again; falling for you, I fractured my wrists.

My head is blooming with flowers and vines, they have wrapped up my brain and eaten me alive. Now all I have the time and capacity to think about is you. It's like the way a vine eats away at brick until the houses break and fall, I am consumed by my own thoughts of you, reminiscing about this morning when I saw you. You make me so happy to think that my head is blooming with flowers and vines, they have wrapped up my brain and eaten me alive.

I WANT TO FEEL
YOU DRIP DOWN ME

i want my legs to be covered in your sweet and sticky,

      honey-coated to the glass so hard you need to scrape

      honey so sickly sweet you lick your finger tips

i want to pass time by counting beads of sweat drip drip   drip

                  resting

                  between you and me

i want to spend hours counting the thoughts on your mind

      counting the things you whispered when

      you thought i couldn't hear

i want to eavesdrop between your toes,

        place myself like jam, like a bunion

        like something you might not actually want

i want to clean off the world from you before you enter the house,

    i don't want you to bring in any toxins,

    i don't want this thing to get poisoned,

    i don't want you to die

so, i wipe you clean with wet naps as you stand in the doorway:

    we leave your shoes outside,

    we leave your clothes outside,

    we leave our brains resting in the vase,

    we leave the germs outside

inside i lick you clean from head to toe before the sacrifice can begin,

    before your insides can come out,

        before i can feel you drip down me

How are you?

The Best Friend who lives far away is not doing well. She hasn't been doing well for a while. The Girl, the best friend of The Best Friend who lives far away, has noticed the unwell but seems frozen. There is too much to say, The Girl justifies, and I do not want to offend. The Best Friend feels lonely, the distance, she says. The Girl and The Best Friend have other friends, but the history is not there. The history is important. The history fills in the silence, the gaps in conversation. The history fills the spaces where The Best Friend cannot speak. The history fills the space where The Girl will not speak.

The Girl thinks about The Best Friend, often. Very often. The Girl talks about The Best Friend and sends well wishes from herself and strangers to The Best Friend. The Girl wonders if The Best Friend feels them. Maybe late at night as she dreams, The Girl sneaks in like the tooth fairy and leaves happiness under her pillow. The Girl thinks about The Best Friend, but she gets too nervous to talk, too nervous to make matters worse, too nervous to lose The Best Friend. So nervous to lose The Best

Friend that The Girl starts to feel like nothing is better than the wrong thing. But isn't nothing wrong, too?

The Best Friend thinks of The Girl often. She thinks about why she has to be the first one to reach out. Why she is always the one to talk more, why she has to bare her heart when The Girl is so quiet and resilient. The Best Friend wonders if The Girl is harboring all the bad in her life. Does one of them need to suffer for the other one to do well? The Best Friend thinks her turn is over, if that is the truth, then it is The Girl's turn to suffer.

The Girl is not doing well. Wasn't doing well before and isn't doing well now. Neither of them are doing well. It is hard to do well when your best friend lives so far away. It is hard to do well when you are nervous that your wellness is not as important as someone else's. The Girl is not doing well, but she is nervous to tell The Best Friend, because she does not want to make a scene. The Girl doesn't want to make this about herself.

The Best Friend and The Girl see each other sometimes and they laugh and smile, but they both seem nervous. Neither of them wants to climb inside each other, they are both scared to bring up the insides. Neither of them wants to do bad anymore. They both want to do well.

Neither of them is doing well.

CLIPPINGS

The echo of your voice mingling with the words from the songs you send me. I can no longer use a toothpick to sort the voices out. You tangle into my own voice, we are submerged in my thoughts. I did not know that clipping your voice box and storing it in my pocket would mean that I could never turn you off; I just wanted to bring a piece of you home, I just wanted to feel closer to you for a moment.

I am afraid you will find where I have hid you, that you may unbury yourself from the contents of my heart and rise up to bring me with you. Fear is not always a bad thing, sometimes it is just the loss of control, but I would trust you to control me. I have thought about the politeness of what is expected, how maybe I should have left my own voice box behind, then I could talk to myself and pretend it was you.

It was the whispering in your sleep that did it. I could hear your murmuring and mumbling and my heart could not take hearing your discontent. I nestled my ear next to your mouth and I waited to hear you say you were happy, I waited for a moment of laughter, I waited for a smile, I waited and then I stopped, I stopped waiting and I cut. If I can cut this out of you and replace it with silence then maybe you will have some peace, maybe I can whisper back to you the nice things you never let yourself hear.

Do you miss the sound of your own voice or are you replaying it in your head? I continue to ignore the texts you send me: Where are you? What have you done with my voice box? Please respond, I just want to hold your hand. I'm calling the police.

But you never call the police.

Instead I find you lingering outside of my home, knocking softly on my window at night as I peer through the glass. I can tell you want to come inside which is why I've installed the cat door, I've even left you instructions: to use this door, please crawl through. I find you lingering in between with the fabric laying on your back, the confusion on your face: why do I want to come in so badly, do I want to find my voice box or do I just want to cuddle? I gesture to you, I pat my leg and hold out treats, I beg you to come through the doorway. You lay down. Again, too nervous to make a decision. I lay next to you and pat your head as you sleep.

It is during these times that I wonder if I should reinstall it. While you are laying on my kitchen floor, softly snoozing, I hold your voice box in place where it used to live and I try to speak in your voice. I say to myself all the things I wish I could hear from you. I whisper to myself as if I am you, as if I haven't hurt you, as if this wasn't my decision. I whisper to you that I am sorry. I eat your voice box.

THE OTHER MAN: I CAN'T BE WITH

I dreamt of you last night. This is not the first time. I dream of you and dream of us and what an us we could be. First: I must unlock these dreams. First: I must kill my husband. First: I dream that he is dead and you, the other man, has been unlocked. First: I must make it reasonable because you live so far away, how could it be that we stumble into each other? First: I must be grieving, I must be in town to grieve, you must meet me at the grieving station.

Then: we can fuck. Then: we can pick up where we left off. Then: you and me can tangle together like a knot of skin and flesh so intertwined that I finally understand what you told me when we were younger.

When we were younger: we were friends who met in class, you older, me younger, only separated by one school year. When we were younger: my best friend tells me you are her neighbor, I tell her I am crushing on you, I am crushed thinking you aren't thinking of me, I am teenage horny for you to notice me. When we were younger: we are dating, I am a shitty girlfriend, you are textbook good; I never understood *textbook*, I wanted a good that resembled anything but a textbook, perhaps I wanted honeycomb good or peppercorn good, anything but textbook, so in return: I am a shitty girlfriend. When we were younger: we break up but we stay friends. When we were younger: we make out in your bedroom, your door is allowed to be closed, you bite me and it makes me even more teenage horny for you to do it again. When we were younger: we are friends who'd like to fuck. When we were younger: we do not fuck; but you tell me that during the few weeks of us dating my mother gave you the sex talk, she told you how to do things well so *my first time would be special and good,* but I was not a virgin when we started dating, my first time was not special or good; you tell me on the roof after we broke up while we are just friends that she taught you some good tricks and now you can make girls squirt and thanks to my mother you are so so so good in bed; this makes me so teenage horny for you I almost scream "Fuck me on this roof," I almost throw you off the roof out of jealousy.

In the middle of our story: I move away from you (not just you but everyone in the area). I move a few states away but we stay in touch because I never stop dreaming about you completely. Though I don't think we were meant to date, meant to be with each other romantically, I think we were meant to fuck at the very least. You are my friend I'd like to fuck. My FILF, my FILTH, my FILTHY little friend that I'd like to see what you can do. So we text and you come visit. Mentally, I am thinking I would like to consummate our friendship, finally. We dare each other to get naked alone in my dorm room. We fall asleep naked. We wake up naked. I can't call into memory your penis so I'm guessing I never saw it. I can call into memory you putting stickers on my naked naked breasts, you touching so lightly my boobies, my titties, my nipples harden at the thought of you.

So: we didn't fuck. And: we don't date.

Rather: I dream of you on and off always. I tell my partner when I do dream of you and they tell me they are weird and entertaining dreams. Neither my partner nor I are dumb to the fact that we can love each other and want to fuck other people. I tell my partner I never got to fuck you but that I am eternally attracted to you. My partner tells me they too have people like that but in regards to themselves. You have my partner's blessing to ravage me, to take me into bed and show me those tricks that you learned, to fuck me so hard and good the image of your dick is engrained in my mind, the touch of your hands branding my skin, the feel of your semen leaking out of me forever drip drip dripping.

Now: I am married. You came to the wedding. It was a beautiful day to get married and I love my partner so so so much that I can't contain the amount of love I have for him. The love I always wanted is the love I have with my partner. Romantically I feel fulfilled and full and so happy. But: that doesn't mean I don't get mid-twenties horny for *other* people. Especially: that doesn't mean I don't get mid-twenties horny for you, still. Still: I ooze horniness for you, my juices exploding in regards to you, sincerely my body is throttling towards you.

I dream of you: I dream of being close to you: I dream of what it would be like to be with you: I dream of the ways in which our bodies find each other again and again: I dream of the world ending and me being with you (my partner already dead, probably killed themselves because the apocalypse is scary): I dream of going to your house and seeing your dad and brother who I hold so much love and care for: I dream of them being happy, we are friends and fucking, happy we are fucking friends: I dream of what it would be like to take this relationship to the next level: but is it possible our next level is not a relationship but just some sex every now and then?

Do you ever think of me? Do you ever dream of me? You've told me before: your girlfriends don't like us talking, they are jealous, they are hive-mind haters of me. I interpret this as: you too dream of fucking me and they can sense that we are two friends who would love to see each other naked and that can be hard to come to terms with if you believe in monogamy or if you believe that to fuck and to date and to be in love is all the same shit. I think: we are smarter than that. I think: we both know you can want to fuck your friend because your friend is just a hottie who makes you laugh and cream your jeans.

I hold so much love for you, SMMM. Smmm, I simmer down to a low temperature: I simmer and cool and laugh: I simmer. But I hold so much love for you and sometimes it comes to a hot steamy boil. You: are such a sweetheart, such a weirdo, such a funny funny guy. You: have always been hot, have always attracted me, have always made my hands ache for you. I: wonder if I will be old-person horny for you after decades pass between us. I: wonder if we will find each other in the apocalypse. I: wonder if you dream of me as much as I dream of you.

But I dream so much for you too: I dream for you to be happy and to find happiness, to find someone who makes you happy and hopefully is not just jealous, to find a love that makes sense for you because you are such a selfless kind person, you deserve the whole world; I dream that you find the whole world and the whole world finds you, to find a world that is crafted to be a home for you, for you to be proud of yourself and know that you are the best kind of person to be.

I just also dream so much of us, the evolving us, the enveloping us, the intertwined us.

But you live so far away. You are just the other man: I can't be with.

Best Friends Never Win

There is a mourning of exes that never were, that is somehow sadder, somehow more sultry than the times in which lives move on from people the world knew were in love. Rather, we were hidden in the depths of bedrooms and linens, lining the hearts of each other through notes and memories, but when the world checks its notes, we never were. That is how you treat it.

I first met Her when we were younger through the force of friendships that lived outside of our own will. She was hopeless from a young age. Drowning in the sorrows of what-ifs and can't-bes, I think this is why we took to each other. There is something romantic in misery, we know it loves company, but we would have rather become one. When I first met Her she was hopelessly devoted to another, to others, to someone who didn't want to love her back. This was her curse, to always be the wanter and not the wanted. She had a knack for finding the girl who was straight and latching on, wanting to suck the life out of her until she could wear her skin and become one, but they didn't love her and they had to remind her. When I first met Her she was hopeful about new beginnings, about the way in which time moves forward that inherently allows for new things to happen, for the past to become more and more and more distant. It was no shock that I was her new beginning.

When Her met me, I was hopelessly following a boy that didn't love me, but knew how to say he did in every way besides his actions (which is to say he could say it with his words). Neither of us were uneducated in the sense that we understood you could be "not straight." Neither of us assumed we were "straight." When Her met me, she told me the words of the language that was not out of reach but somewhere that I was not reaching. Me, hopefully grasping upwards towards the sky and her redirection towards my own pocket where the truth laid like a folded up napkin. When Her met me, I thought of nothing but being with her after we swung on swings together, everyone watching at my own birthday party.

There was a night in the darkness that changed everything for us. The way in which we unfolded and refolded the laundered linings of our bodies, exchanging secret recipes we found hidden in the pockets of our bones, the secret language I found hidden in the folding of her joints. It is easy to romanticize two lesbians fucking under a blanket, but you must remember I was not a lesbian and for Her that was never quite okay enough. Two girls with bones wrapped in cling film, bones gnawing against each other in moist air clogging the ways in which we could breathe each other in. Fogging the route of breath, wanting to suck the souls out of each other, viciously fucking like we were auditoning for a porn we didn't know was being made. Legs and legs and arms and bodies in the middle that felt like butter that had melted and coated the bed.

The downfall of the night was the way in which I wasn't actually, quite technically, almost literally, almost hopeful that I was, but wasn't actually single. There was a man waiting for me on the other side of the metaphorical door that we both knew I now had to leave. Not for Her, but for the sake of not having that man, who was always too nice in a way that was unrelated to me — giving jewelry and diamonds to a girl who never wore a necklace, wouldn't let him put it on, waiting for me in the world that existed outside of this blanket fort, waiting to hear from me to hang out when he didn't know I was already busy fucking my best friend.

This may seem out of time, this may seem out of order, for you my ex-friend, ex-lover, ex-confidante, Her, but I have been dreaming more of you lately and it seems about time that I told you through words of the way in which I will likely always dream of you. Two friends, two lovers, two people attached at the hip and the womb and the mouth and the fingertips, made almost in the perfect pattern, almost matched up exactly, except for all the ways in which we would never agree. Could never agree. Your jealousy took a kingdom to decipher, but I was one girl, scared. That isn't to say I am not to blame. I was kind of a whore. At least to you, I always would be. To this day I hate the word monogamy, the way it feels in the mouth and the way it enforces rules on me that I will not adhere to. I guess this is to say I was more of an attention whore, but you didn't want anyone else to see me. To you, I was hopelessly beautiful, an object of affection, an objectification of your attention, a savored antique that you wanted on the highest shelf, out of reach, to not talk back. But I kept falling off the shelf into the hands of another man, of another woman, of just a friend, but not the kind of friend you wanted me to have. This isn't to say I am not to blame. I did not fall, I jumped.

The last straw for you, I think, was long before you called it quits. Though we fucked and loved and sat like the last two balls alone in a bucket for years after, I think the last straw was the older man. The way in which you saw me melt into him, his temperature hotter than yours but only to you. The way in which I waited for him for too many years. Not alone, not patiently, not even actively (or so I thought), but I did wait until the day in which he wasn't embarrassed of our mismatched numbers to make it official. The one caveat, the one asterisk that made it non-monogamy was that I wouldn't give you up. This was your one condition, if you were going to rent me out, then he must sign on the dotted line that I was not *not* yours. I could not be *just his*. Best friends always kiss, this wouldn't change, you told him. He laughed and agreed, but he didn't know then that best friends always win.

My favorite memory is the one that comes right after my last straw. To be honest, it comes after I forgave you for the straw you took. We were sitting on the porch at a beach house that neither of us were paying for. Rather, we were sitting on the porch at a beach house our friends invited us to. You on my lap, me wrapped around your waist holding you closer to me once again. Me, hopelessly realizing that if I wanted you to stay, I would have to forgive you. You, hopeful that finally I had. I remember the way in which my heart picked up the pace every time I saw your long black hair, always slightly covering the upper left portion of your glasses. When you sat on my lap and I smelled the green apple VO5, my heart told me that it didn't care about any straws, it just wanted to taste the way your lips said "I love you" again. My favorite memory is kissing you again on the porch that nobody really wanted us at anymore — too wrapped up in each other to notice or leave.

The last straw for me, I know now, is when I should have left. I don't regret forgiving you, but I do regret going back. I want to make this clear to you now, I will never think of you as a bad person. I will only think of you in my best memories of us in love, which is likely why I'm dreaming of you now, which is likely why I wish for things to come back in a way that hurts, which is likely why our memories feel painful. The last straw for me should have been when we were both too drunk and I said no. Yes, best friends kiss, best friends kiss and lick and eat each other's teeth. They make out and sweat and suck the tongues out of each other's mouths. Best friends kiss, but they keep their clothes on. I know you say now that you thought it was a game because let's face it, I was kind of into BDSM, I was kind of into saying no and meaning yes, but for me it was the times I said our safe word that you hurt me even more. There is always safety in games that must remain maintained. Best friends are supposed to listen.

I texted you the next day, confused and hurt. I didn't think of you then as someone who wanted to hurt me, but I thought of you as someone who had. I did not wish bad things for you then. Though after you texted the older man I did wish that you would stop. If last night wasn't enough attention, if last night didn't put me back on your shelf, then the ways in which you claimed your ownership over me afterwards certainly did. I used to admire the ways in which your passion drove your decisions, but I did not realize until then that your passion overtook the way we loved each other.

My mother was already dead by this time and I had stopped being straight-edge years before. You were the only person I got drunk with because I always got too honest and sad to remain with anyone but you. When I cried on the toilet, slowly vomiting up the green apple vodka, I told you that I missed my mother and I was wildly in love with you. You always pretended the tears were only for her and not for the way in which I knew our love was built to fall and crumble in the way that shatters both of us.

We already know how the story ends, I kiss you again years after the final straw on the porch with people watching not knowing that we had made up (we didn't even know we were on talking terms by that point). In that moment I forgave your hands for betraying me, I let go of the times I cried by myself unsure of why it had to end like that — love lost due to longing and lust and goddamn silence. In that moment I forgave you for taking back the glasses you gave to my sister on the day of her big lacrosse game even though she didn't have a backup or even any contacts — though I still think it was a dick move. In that moment when our lips touched I felt in my heart that I had never been happier, but secretly in the corner I think my heart knew we would never be forever. Best friends, just for now while we could suppress the past.

There are memories between our final straws and the time we last talked. Most of the memories are good ones, like when we marched in the Pride parade only weeks before they made it legal for us to marry — likely we would have if I hadn't had work that day; memories like when we drove to the city to see Edgar Allen Poe's house or the Eastern State Penitentiary; memories like seeing our favorite bands in concert and meeting your friends who really did like me and think we were the cutest couple. Most of the memories are happy and lovely and make my heart flutter, but every other memory is bogged down with lonely — like when we weren't sure if we should make out in front of the radical church dude because we weren't *technically* dating or like when you got mad at me for the attention I got from guys we didn't know because you always felt like I was asking for it, you always felt like I was the prettier one or like when we fought in the tent in the rain because we wanted things to be like in high school, like before the straws were drawn, like when we were in love inside those folded blankets. There are memories between our final straws and the time we last talked, but they are tainted with the salty taste of inevitable failure.

Sometimes I dream of you, I'm not afraid to tell you that. I dream of the way you used to hold me, the way you made me laugh. Often in these dreams you end up leaving me. Often I wake up with pangs of wanting to love you again, but you never answer my texts — I won't send any more. I wake up thinking of how everything felt abrupt even though we always knew.

All of this isn't to say that I regret the man that I am going to marry, or that I find him to be incorrect or wrong. That would be unfair. I find him to be lovely and perfect. All of this is to say that I will always love you both, lovely and perfect, but that I never trusted you again.

WILTING

My best friend has become quite the bog. She has become such a swamp. Lately, my best friend has filled with water and grass and drowned in the dreams of what she used to be.

We all tried to save her. We all reached out and asked her to please please please reach towards us. We told her to take her hands out of her pockets, we had enough change for her, we could afford to carry her too — the horse we rented could hold us all. We all reached out but we must have mixed our messages because she didn't know who to reach for. She didn't know we had the money. She never knew we rented the horse.

My best friend has become quiet and still in the wake of her death. She has slowed slowed slowed to the last version we all loved of her. For me it is her laughing while we camp, laughing while we drink, laughing while we kiss. For me it is her laughing. It is her being happy and at peace with the world. It is her as I knew her — laughing.

But today I woke up and I opened my phone and I saw the notification: Best friend has turned to bog. I asked my phone what it meant. I saw the response: Best friend is wilted and mold, must find new. I don't want new. I don't want new.

My best friend had become rugged. Had become hard to wear. Had begun to become fragile and small. Lingering inside of my memory is best friend at her fullest, at her happiest, at peace with being a cloud and taking us all for a ride — taking us all to our happy places. My best friend has deflated and crashed.

My best friend has become a bog. Crashed and burned into a bog. Felt like they couldn't climb out of the bog. Stayed and slept in the bog. Made a home in the bog. Is starting a family in the bog.

I've Fallen in Grief

I've been so happy to be in love, I almost forgot what grief was like. I got to, was honored to, was nominated to, fall in love this year and it kept my heart blossoming and blooming. Not only that, but I got to fall in love when I was already in love, both of these loves converging and investing in one another.

I've been so in love, I forgot what in grief felt like. Both taking over your body. Both making you cry. Both making you useless sacks. I've been so in love, I almost couldn't feel when in grief took over.

And now I fall in grief day by day. I've fallen in grief and I can't get up, it is draining me from the cuts on my knees, but I will deflate and bleed out and die. I've fallen in grief and my lovers cannot cure this, their sweet sweet kisses mean everything to me, but grief is blocking them from my bloodstream.

I've fallen in grief. This may be where I die.

TO MEND

Baby Girl

My baby girl is all snuggles. All snuggle snuggles and no grief. My baby girl has never talked back, mostly because she is a cat but also because she understands love. I see other girls, other baby girls and all they can do is talk and talk and talk. Infuriating. I want to tell them all to hush, to settle down, to not worry, to snuggle snuggle and all will be fine.

My darling Cordi never listened. I warned her against her baby girl — human, that darn girl was — I warned Cordi and I told her that if she would get a cat or turn her girl into a cat or manifest a cat into being then she would be all set. But she didn't.

The girl grew and grew and Cordi just broke and broke. I remember the day she was born, it was all fuss fuss hustling and fussing about. That darn girl almost broke Cordi in two, right down the middle from vagina to head. So sensitive she was, Cordi and that girl both. So sensitive at the vagina, so ripe for the picking, so vulnerable.

But the girl grew and grew and I saw Cordi melt and melt. Whenever nights passed and the darn girl would go out and about, not a care in the world. I told Cordi I would follow her, that I could follow her if she wanted. She always said no no there is such a thing as trust but all I thought was that I knew snuggles and snuggles and never had to worry about trust. My baby girl couldn't leave the house if she wanted, couldn't leave if she tried. I never installed the cat door.

I still followed Cordi's girl, though. I knew that her baby girl was too much talk that the trust was lost somewhere along the way. I don't know, maybe she left in the doorway on her way out, all I knew was Cordi needed someone to be suspicious and so I was.

Most nights Cordi's girl would just kind of walk around. Real boring stuff. I would follow a block or two behind, just looking, just thinking, just looking and thinking about the ways in which this girl was all too much for Cordi and I know Cordi was thinking it too. A friend knows her friends and whenever I saw Cordi I could tell how bogged down with girl her face was. How worry would stand right on her shoulders. She never relaxed.

Most nights Cordi's girl would just walk around, but some nights she would meet with strange boys in strange parking lots down strange streets. They always bugged me out and I wish I had told Cordi that. I took lots of pictures, lots of mental pictures, that is. Pictures of the vacant parking lots, pictures of Cordi's baby girl snuggling up on some man that looked way too much like a younger version of her father and I bet she didn't even know that — Cordi or her baby girl — they're both so naive. I even took pictures of Cordi's precious baby girl drinking some alcohol, I have no idea where she got it. Cordi hardly ever drinks and she certainly does measure it, you have to around those girls. That's why I'm so glad my baby girl couldn't drink, she just sits and stares, she's never even asked for any catnip.

Cordi's girl gets so drunk sometimes, so drunk she is hardly walking, but she seems to drag herself about. Sometimes she gets so drunk the boys have to carry her off somewhere else and she is all limp and sad looking, that poor girl with no care, all talk no snuggles snuggles for her mama, she looks like she's giving them all to those boys. And she does! Cordi's girl is all limp

and slippery and she just lets those boys snuggle snuggle up inside of her and I take pictures of it, those mental pictures, of Cordi's baby girl getting all cozied up to, defiled, Cordi's baby girl getting all unzipped and rezipped.

I've thought about stepping in sometimes, believe me I have. But I'm not even supposed to be out here, Cordi didn't even want me out here. I only came out here to make sure I was right about her baby girl, or should I say baby woman. That's right, Cordi's girl is no girl, Cordi's little baby is all woman now full of sharp promises. Oh, but Cordi would have a fit if she found out I went behind her back so I just store up these pictures in case Cordi asks me one day if I ever got the hint that she *did* want me to go and look after her baby girl and then I can say I sure did get the hint and here are all the pictures I took of your baby *woman* Cordi and I sure do think you should have a talk with her about it.

Cordi's baby is so grown up now, she is all stumbles and sag. Sometimes I think Cordi should have fixed her up like I did my baby girl. Before I even got there they knew what to do — she's all fixed, they told me. *Fixed.* She's all sewn up, all stitched up, there's nothing going in or out of there, they assured me. No grandbabies come out of my baby girl, just the way it should be. All baby girl forever, no chance of becoming a woman. I told Cordi before, get your girl fixed before it's too late. *Fixed*, I told her. Fix that girl up and then she can stay baby girl forever. Cordi never listens. She goes on and on about trust and trusting, on and on about *her* baby girl needing *freedom* as if my baby girl gets none. *Freedom*, I tell Cordi, *is relative*. Free in the house is more freedom than just a bedroom. And besides, I always tell Cordi that once a baby girl gets out in the public there is no way she's coming back home.

Cordi's girl always acts the same at home, like she doesn't give all the boys snuggles, like she doesn't drink that poison. I look at her real good whenever I'm over there and I make sure to let her know I'm looking. I'll look Cordi's girl right in the eyes, I look at her like she's a *woman* like I know she's a *woman* and I tell her that I'm watching her. Cordi's girl always giggles, she does. That girl is never serious, she is always all giggles and hair flips. Cordi's girl just looks back at me with her woman eyes pretending to be girl and she just laughs and walks away.

I ask Cordi what she thinks of her baby girl and she always says the same thing, she loves her, but she's *tired*. She says how hard it is to *mother*, especially how hard it is to *mother* a *girl*. She tells me this like I don't understand, like I don't have a baby girl myself. I tell Cordi, all the time I tell her, I tell Cordi that I understand, I understand because my baby girl is just so small she never had a chance out there in the world. Then I tell Cordi that she would be better off keeping her baby girl *inside*, remember I tell her, *freedom is relative*. I don't bother talking about fixing her up anymore, I know that girl is more woman now so I don't even mention it. I wonder if Cordi can tell, if she can sniff out the ways in which her baby girl is baby woman, unhinged.

Cordi's been getting mad with me lately and I just can't get why. I go over there and I offer my advice and Cordi gets all snippy with me about my baby girl just being all *cat* and no *hassle*. I tell Cordi she doesn't know, she doesn't understand, she doesn't even have a cat, she is all *human* and no *hassle*. I don't even mean to but in the rage of it all I tell Cordi about her baby girl being no baby no more. I throw it in Cordi's face about the *fixing*, about how my baby is always girl and hers is just a lousy woman. Cordi gets real mad at that, she is all anger and no fun and I start to feel kind of bad but then Cordi goes to yell at her baby and I know we're done fighting. Cordi yells at her baby *woman* and I know this was all about me being right and her being angry at her *girl,* at her *woman.*

Cordi yells at her girl so much I can hear it from downstairs and I hear her girl yelling, I hear her sounding so sad it seems like she may never recover. I hear those two *women* yelling and hollering and I hear pushing and shoving and all sorts of sounds so I just kind of leave. I leave and I wait until Cordi gives me a call a few days later, waiting just enough time to let the dust settle.

Cordi calls and finally I go back over and I ask about her baby *woman* and Cordi tells me they sorted it all out, but she is real sorry about the *hassle* she caused me and I know she is. Cordi tells me she took care of her *woman,* she stuffed her all back up with sweetness. Cordi tells me she understands being a good mama, just like me and she is so thankful to have *me* and boy that is just so sweet to hear. Cordi tells me how I was so right about the *fixing* and that's why Cordi's girl is all stuffing and cotton now. She's lost her way, that darn girl. Got so lost she found herself stuffed up with cotton where her insides used to be. Now she's all cuddles, and snuggle snuggles.

YOU WANT TO
FEEL SPECIAL

you want to feel special,

that is what you always told me, anyway. that if you found some way to be special, to appear special, to soak up all of the specificities of the world and embody them all that you would then feel complete and whole

you told me this as we drove through the fields, as we kept driving, as the car hurtled us forward, you whispered to me that you would be special if things were wrong with you; that you might feel whole if the sepsis has leaked into your bones.

i thought this was what you wanted, when you told me that your muscles had dried and shriveled and you were stuck stuck stuck,

you want to feel special.

you want to feel as special as you can, you want the looks and the oglers and the way that people stare into you and through you as if you are a window

but you want to be pretty, you screamed at me *do i look pretty do i look pretty do i look pretty do i look pretty is there anything about me that looks pretty*

and the tears gliding down your face through your shirt glistened like dew: you're beautiful i told you.

but you want to feel special, *and god who isn't pretty now-a-days?*

you want to be special so you hide inside the corners of sauces and soups trying to wrangle the bones flavoring the sauce, *i'm rebuilding from the ground up,* your muscles groan and convulse and you try to turn from side to side

you become the wooden spoon stirring my pot

you pick at the parts that drift by and snatch them one by one: carrot, turnip, bone, bone, bone, string of fat seeping to the surface, foam beginning to gurgle, bone, bone,

you leave dozens of carcasses at my feet, mostly immobile, any slight imperfection and i hear you crying from the bathroom *why can't i be pretty?*

do i look pretty? do i look pretty? you want to leave this cycle but there is only one type of special you can see the world seeing you in and you want to run from it. you want to conjure the image of the most special person in the whole world, you want to become Jesus without the stunts, you don't need to walk on water because everyone knows you are special.

so you wait in the soups and sauces and you collect more: heads of turnips and carrots and radishes and you connect these to the bones that pile up, the cartilage only half dissolved, you call out of work again, if i'm being honest you might not even work there anymore.

you spend your days stapling together the bones and the turnips and the fat. you spend your days trying to build the new you. you spend your days almost succeeding, almost breathing, almost allowing your body to rise, but as your new body begins to stand you always find something wrong with you. you never feel special.

you tell me that jobs don't matter because once you are so so so pretty the world will open up and you'll burn that place to the ground and everyone there will burn and die and then you can start on your children. your crispy children losing scales of skins. your wonderful children waiting for you to craft them, to give them life.

you tell me that once you finish your new body, once you find the right chicken carcass to hold your turnip head, you will have the spare time to pick the crisp skin off the people you've burnt down and then you will have the time to separate muscle from bone and charred remains from teeth and then you will have the time to create more pretty pretty people

(just not quite as pretty as you)

do i look pretty? do i look too young to be a mother? do you think they look like my sisters? if i was outside of the store, do i look young enough that people may think i'm stealing them?

your smile is never like anyone. i tell you again and again that your smile is so so special, so so beautiful and handcrafted, so so pretty. everytime i say this you hide your face

BIRD SEED

He was shedding like a shag carpet, I could feel traces of him every step I walked. The old him molting his skin, tears and tears of his happyunhappyhappyunhappyunununhappy self.

"When did it happen?" I asked him, "When did you begin to pluck all your feathers to become a dying wilting bird?"

He couldn't manage an answer, he nodded and walked away.

I find feathers in the woods of happy times and cherry trees and I staple them back on. If only I could find other happy memories to make him forget that unhappiness can exist. I would pluck them out of the dreams at night, roaming from house to house to find one more to tuck away in the fold of his knees or the crevice behind his ear (quietly whispering to smile to smilesmilesmile if he just gave us a smile then his face will freeze that way and his brain will freeze that way and happiness will finally know his name).

He is uneasy in the face of freshness, untrusting when it comes to smiles, the people who come in with good faith are nothing more than hopeless or idiots. I cannot say I disagree but I can live in the gray area, he can live in unhappy or happy.

He has lived in unhappy for far too long. I know he is becoming enveloped feet first. At night I uncover his feet to find them beginning to blacken, beginning to shed toenails and cuticles, beginning to replace his blood with vinegar. I chip away at the rotted leaves and water him with sunshine. I hold a flashlight under his blanket so he can try to find a way to some light source, he can try to find a way toward something not blackened to the brim, boiling over on the stove.

I blow bubbles his way on the streets. Following behind him so he can catch a glimpse of whimsy. With these moments I can sense him trying to hold it in. I do not know if this is unhinged happiness or the final snap of his neck.

I go to the birds at parks and try to find the happiest ones, the ones who are smiling freely, the ones that seem to know where the good seeds are. I find them and I shoot them and I cook them until they become a dust. This is the dust I shower him with. Day or night. I will sprinkle him with the cremated remains of happiness. Cooking them down to something he knows what to do with.

THE ACTS OF RITUAL

ACT I

We will now introduce the main character. However, she does not have a name. This is because she lost it long ago. She may have set it down in the woods for resting. Perhaps even, she loaned it to a friend. Whatever the case, it is gone and it won't come back.

In this act we will need to give you the background of something. That background may be that before there were people, there were only lobsters. These lobsters were really, really big. Quite huge, even. However, they became bored of living and shrunk until other things could emerge from within them. One of them must have given birth, most likely the largest one — harboring babies inside her stomach. They revolted as the lobsters shrunk and shrunk, losing their power. That may be how she was born.

ACT II

This is not the middle. Not yet, anyway. We promise you more words before we reach that point.

She is a classic damsel creating distress. I think it stems from distrust. Daddy issues. He abandoned her long ago, she still had a name then. He kept her siblings, all of them besides her. He keeps her sister Margo in a locket around his neck. Sometimes when he is lost he will open her up for directions like a GPS. Margo is useful. He keeps her brother Jeffrey within the laces of his shoes. Mainly this is to walk all over him, but he knows that in exchange for this pleasure there will come a day when Jeffrey will take over and hang him by his neck, shoes dangling in his face. It has been said this day will not come for fifty more years and of course, Daddy will think he really won. He keeps the mother alive and well. She has no memory of children, she only has regret for never having one. She finds creatures in the woods to nurse back to health. She has never found her unnamed daughter. Daddy wouldn't let her.

As most middle children are, our damsel is blamed for the disaster that has amplified the distress. Most likely it is the regret of having two before the pleasure of three. In a Christian family they then can pretend they have birthed the holy trinity. The father, the son, and the holy ghost. However, they are atheist converts — it happened after her. Right in the middle of birthing the trinity, they decided to give up hope. They would say she took it from them.

Our damsel is beautiful, as they always are. She looks exactly like you think — pretty. Most likely when you stumble upon her you would think she is dumb, because she doesn't have to be smart with looks like that. Like damn, she could be a model or maybe an actress — those are just careers for vacant people like her.

However, there is a difference between vacancy and dumbness. She feels very little, but she thinks very much. Really, if you read her diary you would think she was ugly, because girls with a brain like that can survive off it. They don't need good looks, because they're really self-sufficient. She's the total package.

Besides the distress she always brings.

ACT III

In this act, the action will start. We will tell you about how this girl wants revenge. We would like to tell you she also wants a family and to save her brother and sister — even her mom. But she does not want that. The truth is that she didn't like her family even before this all happened. Even before she was left in the woods as a sacrifice to nothing. She was already planning to leave. Really she would have.

But they got to her too soon. Daddy saw her packing her bags and you know how men can be. So he tied her to a horse and dragged her to the woods where there were creepy stones and sticks. Really, he looked like he had done this once or twice before because he didn't even have to look for it or bring up directions. We're pretty sure he thought she was a whore because he made this whole big deal about not letting any slutty sluts inside his home because even if they were atheist, you've got to have some sort of decency — like, come on. So he sang a weird song about purity and bliss and now she could die and be revirginized in the next place her stupid slutty body went and then he gutted her like a pig, but he would say he gutted her like a whore (which looks a lot like gutting her like a pig).

Needless to say, she wasn't a slutty slut, she wasn't even a regular slut. Sure, she liked to walk around naked and tease men, but women are women and they can do as they please. We're not sure how much you know about sacrifice, but you really need to get things right or your daughter of distress will only become more godly and less humane.

But she is patient. She is so goddamn patient you wouldn't even know she existed unless you read about her in some story, because she is still waiting for the right time to gut her stupid father like the useless boy he is.

As for her family, the others that are locked in dreams, not quite in this world, she is debating what to do with them. She kind of likes to live in the moment, so I think she might wing it and see how she's feeling when it happens.

ACT IV

Oh crap, we promised you action. Well the backstory kind of had some, so I guess we at least half delivered. You'll have to wait for more. We want to make sure you understand this lady, and it can be hard to do. So often we rely on names of girls so that we can associate them with other girls and then we can make our final decision. This isn't possible, unless you know a girl who lost her name eons ago after her daddy gutted her like a whorey little pig. Then this girl is probably similar to that one.

We would like you to feel sympathy for her, and for all girls, really. She didn't deserve to die (or to be on the brink of death and brought back by a botched ritual). Sure, she wasn't necessarily the easiest to live with but middle children never are. They always think they are the short straw and deserve a fucking break, but honestly, she kind of did. Her other siblings used to pawn off their chores to her on the cheap and whenever she needed to borrow a few bucks they would hike the interest rates way up. Like for instance, Margo once needed to borrow ten dollars from Jeffrey to go to the movies with her friends and Jeffrey was like, okay, I'll give you ten, but you'll need to pay me back eleven, and Margo was like, deal; but then when this damsel needed to borrow five just to make up the difference because she really wanted to get some tickets to a concert, Jeffrey charged her a vig of ten percent daily and she also had to do his chores for a week without pay from him. So really, she was the short straw and she was really tired of it. Margo and Jeffrey always looked out for each other and she just wanted to feel for once like she had someone looking out for her.

This doesn't mean, however, that she was always in the right. People never are. Don't misread all that nonsense that says anyone is ever really truly good — they probably wrote it themselves and that is a biased source. When she was little, she used to spit in her parents' cereal whenever they asked her to make breakfast. She also used to cut Margo's nails too short and paint them in really unflattering colors (Winters cannot pull off orange). And there was the one time she burned down a church because her ex-boyfriend's dad was the pastor. Needless to say, she has a complicated past, but I, for one, am on the side of her not deserving the death her daddy attempted to thrust upon her.

ACT IX

Do not throw a fit. We can order these however we want. They contain the same truth whether they come now or they come later. Either way, they will come.

This act is a spell, a sermon, a conjure.

Some say that you can find her. It will always be deep in the woods — night or day — but always by that altar with the stones and sticks. You must take your father there and beat him to death and then beat him more. You must roar to the matriarchy.

At least that's what the rumors say.

ACT V

Like most men, Daddy hated being wrong.

There was this one time that Margo had won a bet about who would win the Superbowl and Daddy locked her in her room for three days and forbade her from watching sports again.

Our damsel knew she needed to show him that he couldn't even kill his own daughter correctly. Our damsel knew that the secret to his distress would be living with the fact that he was an amateur ritualist. Nothing would hurt him more.

This was her plan: She would break into her old home and sneak into the bed of her daddy and cuddle up next to him. When he awoke, thinking his dumb wife had stumbled into the wrong room (they slept in separate bedrooms, mainly because she snored like a wildebeest), he would turn and see the person he had hated the most was actually alive. When he turned, she would stand above him and as he went to stand up, he would find that he couldn't move because she had laced his evening tea with some kind of tasteless tranquilizer she ordered online. Then she would tie his hands and legs to his bed and sing him a song that she was in the midst of writing, about how great women are and how much he sucks at murder. Then she would bring in his wife, her very own mother, and she would reveal to her that she was her child and as her mother began crying and wondering if she was right, our damsel would cut her head off with a butcher's knife (because they look really cool). The last thing to do then, would be to feel out the moment and decide what to do with her siblings. Leave them alive, leave them trapped, break them to pieces, or return them to life.

INTERMISSION

This is the song she wrote:

Deedaleedee deedaleedoo

Men smell like shit and look like poo

Deedaleedum deedaleedamn

I'm so glad I'm not a man

I'll gut my father, better than he gutted me

I'll piss in his face and cut his knees

I don't give a care in the world

That's why I'm a modern girl

ACT VI

This is what happened:

As she snuck inside her home, she hid in her old bedroom, now made into her mother's crafting and eBay selling room. She began to cry. She hadn't realized that she missed her mother. She had missed the way in which she braided her hair and made her oatmeal. She hated the way in which she had only become an extension of Daddy, but she missed the times Mother was a woman who had children. She missed the times when mother was Mother and she was Child.

After crying for a few hours, she finally heard the tea kettle ring and she snuck into the kitchen to tranquilize her father. She hadn't realized, however, that now her mother also drank tea. So she just spiked them both to make sure. She didn't want to half-ass this ritual of freedom she made for herself. As Daddy finished his tea, he went to bed and fell asleep. Then she crawled into bed and waited a few minutes, but as she was going to wake him, Mother walked into the room (almost limping which must mean the tranquilizer did work). She was so confused, but sometimes kids really are the downfall of marriage.

As her mother began falling into bed she shrieked because to her, some strange young lady was in bed with her husband and of course this woke Daddy up. Our damsel stood up and moved to the end of the bed and Daddy looked at her, mesmerized. "Who are you?" he said.

"You know who I am. I'm your daughter." This is when her mother really started losing her shit and crying a really ugly cry with heavy breathing and snot.

"I wear my daughter around my neck, you are not her."

"I'm the one you tried to kill. Remember Daddy? You can't even murder correctly."

"I fear your memory fails you." Our damsel was really confused as to where and when Daddy thought he was and why he was talking like that, "I have only ever slaughtered a whore, not a daughter."

She chuckled a really sultry and sexy chuckle that would have made everyone cream their jeans, "I was no whore Daddy, I was a virgin. That's why you have to be a bit more careful when choosing your ritual."

There was a mixture of anger and fear and some really rapey eyes that crossed his face. Her mother was still on the floor in an emotional lump, but this was the first time he tried to stand. And he did. There was then a mixture of confusion and fear that crossed our damsel's face, the distress started to leak in. Daddy threw his locket on the floor.

"I was very careful young lady. I chose a whore ritual for a whore girl and I won't be told any differently." Our damsel started freaking out and running to the other side of the room. That's when Margo crawled out of the locket: arm, arm, head, torso, leg, leg. She took the blanket hanging off the bed and strangled her father. Our damsel grabbed the shoelaces out of his shoes and tied them around his neck. The laces transformed from lace to limb and Jeffrey emerged, finally free. He wrapped his hands tighter, the blanket tighter, hands tighter, the blanket tighter until Daddy turned blue.

The mother lay on the floor clenching Daddy's dead body. "What the fuck?" she cried and cried and cried until she cried out all her liquids. A lump of a mother on the floor.

ACT VII

You are probably thinking we should wrap this up now that Daddy and Mother are dead, but you should really calm down.

Let's recap who is alive: all the siblings. This was the last option our damsel was leaning towards when thinking about what to do with them (re: the interest rates, the chores). After their parents were dead, they all just kind of stared at each other.

"Well, thanks I guess." Margo said, not really looking at anyone.

"Oh yeah, thank you guys for helping me kill him."

"You're welcome." Jeffrey said, a little too quickly.

"Well I guess I better go." Our damsel started towards the door and her siblings followed her. For some reason, the front door had stayed open since she came in and the house was really cold. They all shivered a little.

Margo said, "I mean, you can stay. I guess we've inherited the house so we can make room for you. We'll just have to think of what to tell the neighbors, but it shouldn't be too hard."

"I totally would, but I think I need to spend some time by myself. You guys should totally keep the place though. Maybe do some painting, open up the walls. You know, open concept."

"I think I'd be pretty good in construction." Jeffrey said. Everyone was getting kind of awkward.

"Well, thanks you guys. Really." She made her way through the doorway.

Margo called out, "You're welcome back anytime, Damsel."

ACT X

The magic has leaked out.

ACT VIII

So there you go — she has a name. Maybe you even guessed it! Damsel brought the distress with her, but she always took it when she left. And sometimes on Sundays, she even goes over for a family dinner now that Jeffrey is out of jail. None of them had really thought of finger printing since they had been locked in objects or exiled to the woods. It turns out he was actually really good in construction and since Margo and Damsel testified that he was acting in self-defense, he only got two years. Now he owns a business and lives in the house. Margo lives next door with her wife and children (only two, thank goodness).

Damsel lives in the woods still. But not in a creepy way. She lives by herself with her pet cat in a cabin. She only lives about forty minutes down the road, but those are the forty minutes that keep her feeling like she is a person and not just some girl who needed her siblings' help. She plays that night back in her mind and she thinks about the way in which she may be dead without Margo. She thinks about the way in which Margo didn't even hesitate, she really just started killing their dad, which makes Damsel feel really close to her. Sometimes, even, she thinks about her mother and how useless she had become; often she thinks this was the warning, the real death of her seeing her mother cry herself asleep forever. Mostly, she thinks about the way she will always be alone. Always in her house with a cat. Always a virgin.

TO BECOME

MY BARREN WASTELAND

the soft gentle touch of my hand on my own vagina sings me to sleep at night. when i rest my eyes and close my brain, my hand wanders through my own body; i dream of wearing myself like a sleeve, of my arm disappearing inside of me, the jungle of my hairs pulling and keeping me settled on myself. i dream of touching myself.

you asked me if i wouldn't mind messing around, if maybe i had thought about playing with shape, if only i would shave shave shave myself down to the nub; and for you. i would have done anything. i tried to shape and center a triangle pointing to my holes, for you, you can use any of them, you can fill in any holes you may like. you can color me in, outside the lines.

you didn't need to keep asking, i could tell by the way your tongue drew lines on me — avoiding avoiding avoiding each pube it came in contact with, your tongue gagging and coughing as it found a stray hair, your tongue puking into my cunt as it realizes the hair still remains.

so i bought a straight razor, i bought wax strips, i bought every possible thing to rip the hairs from my cunt so your tongue could roam freely. i used tweezers to get the edges, to pluck the strays, to gently scrape open the ingrown hairs (only a drop or two of blood) and pull them from my insides, as long as they could grow, i kept them all intact.

sentimentalism strung me up from my throat. i keep each hair i have ever taken out, i cannot bear to separate from them. my children. i grow them and i birthed them and i kicked them out.

and thank goodness i did. it was never enough for your slimy tongue. no matter how far down i dug, there always seemed to be lingering hair or veins or loose organs seeping to the surface, filling my vagina with more and more vomit, eating out my own dinner.

———

it was late at the bar when i met you. when you met my eyes and kissed my nose. how romantic, how new, how absolutely magical to have a kiss kiss kiss planted into my ski-slope nose, how did you even find it, please never let go, eat my nose until you shit it out.

but you didn't like smooth. you told me it was weird how translucent my skin had become, that you didn't like how you could see through my vagina into my body into my organs into the cells that keep me alive. you rummaged through my cabinets and broke all my glass. you found my duct tape and tried to tape my vagina closed, tape the skin back together, but your touch was too hard, the blood soaked through the adhesive and the tape diaper you made me fell off.

that was when you found it. hidden in my bathroom, behind the electrical box, inside a safe with a key (the key hidden under my bed in the false trap board), you found my jar of pubic hair. you dumped it all on my bed, each hair that i carefully plucked floated into the air, a fog of hair i sucked into my lungs. you grabbed my stapler. you spent no time holding me down as i tried to tell you it will grow back, it just might take some time. you spent no time telling me you didn't have another minute, you wanted to be inside of me but you can't fuck someone with a cunt like mine, not like this. you sat on my face and held down my hands with your legs and you placed some hair on my hood and shoved the stapler into my body, staple digging deep inside, closing the gap between hair and skin, hair and skin now coated in blood, oozing and dripping mixing with my cum. you spent no time repeating the process: a fist full of hair, a couple of staples, you sat back harder and harder onto my body, your ass suffocating my face, you shouting eat my ass while i make you perfect. me always so obedient.

and i never hear from you again. the pubes all fell out, of course. they were never meant to be stapled, they were never made for force. my vagina oozed puss for days as it scabbed over the staples, i used my tweezers to carefully pull them out, to grab them and rip, dreaming of smoothness again.

so i go back to bars. chronically lonely. i look for you in corners, who else am i supposed to look for? who else am i supposed to live for? i checked under the cushions, all of them, i asked people to move, i told them i may have lost my phone, that i just needed to check. they all oblige.

———

i lift each cushion, my vagina aching aching aching, begging me just to let it heal. i pull you out by the scruff of your neck, shoved deep deep deep inside the couch at the back of the room. that's where i found you, something shiny and new, someone with eyes so sad i knew i had to take you home. my eyes leaking the whole way home; one hand on the wheel, one hand on the jar catching each tear.

and i bring you back to my house; i draw you a bath and use my body to test the temperature, my tears always the perfect temperature for you. you're shivering in the corner, you look so lovely, so terrified. i stroke your head and tell you that you don't have to worry, i've gotten rid of all the staples in the house, i threw out all the wax strips, i don't even have my jar of pubes anymore. i place you in the bath and let you float.

i wait in my bed for you as you clean yourself up, no rush no rush no rush.

you come to cuddle. you've brought your needle and thread, the ones you carry around to stitch yourself back together in emergencies. you tell me that you reached in my drain and you found the missing pieces, you tell me that you could tell i was feeling incomplete. the look in your eyes made me cry, but it is now your turn, you tell me; you fill the bathtub with your tears for me, you knew i was missing what could make me whole. you show me the fist full of pubes that you snaked out of my drain, they are damp and small, curling into the crevices of your hand.

i lay on my back and close my eyes as my pelvis floats to the surface and you thread my pubic hair back onto my cunt. i close my eyes and dream of your lips as you caress mine, you lick the thread before you loop it through the needle, you kiss my pubes before you loop them through my body, you bandage up my body as i fall asleep and kiss every inch of my newly furnished cunt as i begin to dream.

i dream of you, of who you'll be when i wake up next to you. my sleeping body can feel yours lying next to me, you rest your head on my chest and close your eyes. i meet you in our dreamscape. we hide in between the cushions.

SIZE OO

She had always hoped that one day her feet would grow big enough for her to stop falling down. It seemed as though she was so top heavy that her size double zero feet couldn't carry her. She spent a lot of time hiding. Hiding from her parents who wanted to take her shopping. Hiding from her classmates. Hiding from her own feet, trying to set them aside until they behaved.

Her hands always looked the same. There isn't much to do with them though, when you can't stand, can't walk, can't find the ability to go anywhere. There were times in the space before now when she would be seen in public with her parents or like the times when she went to school. Quickly — as though her body grew and her feet only seemed to get swallowed up — she realized her dreams would only be a memory. She always thought that maybe she could be a potter, but the foot pedal was too big for her feet. It always tried to eat them, tried to beat, tried to suffocate and kill them. Now she stayed in her room home-schooling herself. She only came out when her parents were at work. She would roll around the house, room to room, inching up and down the stairs for snacks and drinks and youthful fun.

But she always knew at 5pm she would lock herself back upstairs. Just like Rapunzel, but instead of long hair, it was small small feet.

She had heard on the news of the amazing foot surgeon named Dr. Foot Surgeon and booked an appointment immediately. She had heard Dr. Foot Surgeon had a way of dealing with feet. Of feeling the feet. Of tying them up and making them look like someone else's feet, someone who had feet people could respect. She couldn't ever find a way to fly out to meet him. She used to use a wheelchair, but that was when her feet were a size much bigger than now. That was when she was a size three. Now if she used a wheelchair, she always seemed to get caught in the wheels, her tiny feet flapping backward and hiding in the screws and bolts. Even if she could get to the airport, they would never let her fly with those feet. There was something suspicious about them. They were too small to seem as though they belonged to her. They needed to be declared. They are seen as something that promised that things were hiding in there. Bugs and mites and drugs and fights. She swore, swore, swore she wouldn't smuggle anything. No, not anymore. But she always did. She barely had any feeling left in there, people would cut them open and hide their dime bags and sheets of acid in between her toes, under her nails, even between her tendons. No, no she could not fly.

She emailed Dr. Foot Surgeon and asked him if he could come to her, told him that long distance would not work out. She cried and begged and honestly seemed pretty desperate. Fine, he said. Send me pictures and I'll see if I can make it. She took 134 pictures of her feet and the webbing and the toes. Her foot measured in total to 2.89 inches long and each toe was webbed to the other with small incisions on each padding. It seemed like she had zippers holding the toes together. Her toenails were half an inch thick, mostly piled with things she didn't have the password for. Always stuck, always stuck, always sticking right where they are, well-behaved. There was a layer of crust on the bottom of her feet that seemed to be callused tissue with a slight bit of mold. It created a smell that reminded everyone of burnt quiche that had expired two weeks ago. Dr. Foot Surgeon could not smell them, though.

When he received the pictures, Dr. Foot Surgeon thought it was a prank. He emailed her that he was not amused and blocked her email. She cried. A lot. She cried so much her feet couldn't hold themselves down and they kept floating to the top, reminding her of what a failure she had become. She thought she had finally gotten out of her pain, out of her feet into a pair that looked like a size seven, size nine at most. She wanted to paint her toes and feel refreshed, but whenever she tried, the nail polish seemed to bubble and boil and burn away. She knew then that no matter what, she would need to meet the doctor, no matter what, she needed to be a person who had a life that involved more than squirming on the ground. She hired a hitman to find Dr. Foot Surgeon and bring him to her. The hitman said that wasn't what hitmen do and recommended a bounty hunter. She told the hitman she had no idea where someone would go to hire a bounty hunter and reminded him of the useless feet she has that impeded her from going out and looking for a bounty hunter — for some reason the ability to hire hitmen was much more attainable than bounty hunters. The hitman emailed her a link to his five most recommended bounty hunters including pictures, zodiac signs, and pricing. She knew the person she chose would have to be quick (out goes Contestant Five who wore tactical boots in every picture, which must've weighed him down). She knew they would have to be strong (out goes Contestant Two who looked like they might've been doing heroin as a side gig). She knew they would have to be bold and bright (out goes Contestant Three who included in his bio that he was neither bold nor bright). She knew they would have to have an opening that week (out goes Contestant One who was booked for another month). She knew it had to be Contestant Four, which was all the better, because he looked like the Prince Eric type that was down to save stranded ladies, even if they had tails and no feet.

After a week-long email exchange, the bounty hunter accepted the job and spent six days finding, kidnapping, and ultimately killing the Dr. Foot Surgeon. It turned out that the bounty hunter had lied on his application because though he was bold and fast, he lacked bright and strong, which resulted in blunt force trauma to the head. The bounty hunter knew the least he could do was bring back Dr. Foot Surgeon's doctor feet, but due to the lack of strength, he realized the least he could do was actually just leave the body intact where it was. By the time the bounty hunter conjured the courage to tell her what had happened, he knew it had been too long. Besides, he didn't even have any feet to offer her. Of course, he considered giving her his, but he still needed them to bounty hunt in the future (that is, of course, assuming that her low rating wouldn't impact future jobs too much. He could always lower prices, run a flash sale, he reminded himself). The bounty hunter had three months worth of piled up emails from her asking where the doctor was, asking for a refund and threatening to call the cops. After going through the emails, the bounty hunter knew exactly what to do, so he dressed up like a doctor and went to her house.

She opened the door, excited that she would finally be able to stand. Finally, she could do the wave and clap without falling down. Finally, she thought, she could go to the mall. She opened the door and asked, "Where's the doctor? Why are you dressed up like a foot surgeon?" The bounty hunter never considered the fact that his application came with a headshot and his immediate reaction was to knock her out. Learning from his mistakes with Dr. Foot Surgeon, he used his hands and no bats. Thankfully, it was easy because she had no balance due to her foot size. The bounty hunter thought of the reputation that all bounty hunters get, how heartless and money focused they are. He knew he didn't want to give her a refund, but he also knew the doctor would never come.

When she finally woke up, she started crying. She read the note that the bounty hunter left saying that he was sorry he knocked her out and he was also sorry he killed the doctor and he was also sorry that he couldn't give her a refund and he was sorry that he pretended to be a doctor and he was sorry he waited three months to get back to her and he was sorry he didn't believe her about her feet and he was sorry about her feet in general and that maybe he could take her out sometime. Because congratulations, he amputated both feet and now she could use a wheelchair or get a bionic leg or two bionic legs and he hopes she's happy in the future.

Mimed Lives

The reason I died the first time was due to politeness. Usually with girls it always is. A relentless need to please that we get closer to killing with each generation.

The second time was worse, it was my own weakness. Trapped in a weaker body — when the stronger you are, the more power you hold.

The third, I was finally the killer. There is never enough space for women in the murder scene but that does not stop us from doing the murdering. There is something much more personal about a slow and painful death; up close and personal like crawling into the cavity of your ribs after creating enough space for me to fit.

I think this happened because I had finally reached my limit. Always trapped in the body of a woman in a world that only respects the body of a man. Wandering through bodiless people, trying on skins and shins and hiding in the crevices of the people who would let me in.

The fourth time, I died of old age. It took about ninety years of solitude and hopelessness before my heart became too sad to hold itself together.

The fifth time was suicide. It always is. By then we know better than to think of the future.

I made an appeal before the sixth time, in hopes of shortening my sentence within this body but as usual for women it was rejected.

The sixth time, I joined a cult and let them tell me what to do. Too tired to hold myself together, already withering away at the core.

The seventh time, I had a baby and told the baby that it would be the death of me; that when the winter came and the power was shut off to eat my body and sleep in my skin. This was the only death I loved.

The eighth time felt like an eternity, but it was only three days. Medicine cannot always help the babies who were not baked enough.

The ninth time will hopefully be the last. The last body of a worn-out girl that I have to wear, have to lug around, have to drag behind me like a mop too wet to carry. I am hoping that this time I go out through rebellion. Off to the guillotine or hung out to dry, maybe even burned like a witch. The ninth time, I will go out in a blaze of glory and will sacrifice myself to womankind.

LEAKING

I don't want to leak out my memories onto your pillow, I've already left so much of me there. At night I can feel my dreams crawl out and inject themselves into your side, I can feel the veins of the pillows pulsing through to each other. I can't afford to lose more of me to your sheets, washed away when laundry day comes.

I try shoving toilet paper in my ears, but the roll never fits. I try to choke down a paper towel holder to furnish my body for you, please clean up after yourself, try not to make a mess. No matter how many paper products I fill myself with, I can feel them all spill out on your bed, I can feel them crumble and mold before my head hits the pillow.

I try not to think of things I want to keep hidden but of course, then, that is all I will think of. I don't want you to see my high school fights or the fear of losing a friend group that you've never met. I want to hide away all the feelings of not being enough in school and shove it under the rug where I keep my feelings of not being enough for you. I super glue the edges to make sure none of them can escape.

But that doesn't stop your crowbar.

The way your hand traces my body, I ooze with wanting, I drip with secrets, I am soaked with impatience. Touch me again and I'll lose all my insides. If you linger over me then I might just emulsify. Then you can wash me out of your sheets.

GIRL-Y

My face is molding clay and I have been trying to massage out the kinks. I can feel the tension holding, refusing to relax, refusing to be something that is not completely and always crinkled in stress. I've watched videos and read how-tos: how to get rid of your stress, how to change your face from wrinkled and sad to happy and free, how to unfold your face, how to turn from stone to wet wet clay.

My face is starting to melt and crumble under the weight of my soggy hands. I've never been delicate, I've never understood how softness works. I think of the times I've disconnected clit from vagina trying to find any amount of pleasure, any amount of clarity, but my fingers are so so aggressive so so angry so so overwhelmed with femininity. What does it mean to be girl-y? What do girl-y girls do? Do they know how to please themselves, how to cum, how to massage themselves and relax and not stress?

I am collecting clay from the bogs of towns. Trying to find enough clay to reconstruct a face that knows how to re-lax. A face that can come un-done. Perhaps un-hinge and open and let out the bad bad thoughts. A face that I can air out once a week to let the smell out, light a candle and refresh the space.

My body is flesh flesh fleshy flesh. It aches with human-ity. There's not enough clay in this world to craft a new one, not one that I could love. I dip my body into bogs and cast clay into the shell of what I used to be, but it comes out in one big lump like a candle that someone has burned down.

My body is fleshy and my face is shocked in time, frozen as a clay cast of stress, my muscles carved to be something so un-re-laxed. My face is molding clay, but my hands are clumsy, so clumsy, they do not know how to create anything. My body is not femi-nine enough to create life, I am not God, just a girl who cannot re-lax. A girl who refuses to calm-down. A girl stuck frozen in time time time.

People are trying to help. People are telling me less screen-time as if the world happens off-line. As if the world could unfold in any way that does not furrow my brow. As if that world could exist and people would still somehow manage a sense of being un-stressed.

I do not think these people understand what it means to be made of bog, they do not think about the people who are not all flesh. Only my lower half, I try to tell them. People with their brains, girls with their girl-y-ness. I am just girl, half bog sculpture, half flesh. Not all of me adds up.

I am trying to re-lax, trying to be-come something else. I fear I may have to get rid of the clay, throw the whole bog out. I fear I may become half fleshy flesh, half vacancy.

YOU'RE MAD!
(SCIENTIST)

I don't know who the surgeon is anymore: you or me. I'm not sure who is making the stitches, the incisions, the symmetry in comparisons. All I can feel is my insides left out in the open; skinned off of me like a moist skeleton, shivering in the wind, shivering so hard I might fly away.

But I can see the body you are keeping in the corner. Grafting my skin onto a body more perfect, a mind more gentle, a frame more enticing. I can see the body twitch and ache, craving more of you, more of your touch, more of your *specialized skills*. You, the god to the body you are making out of me. Me, the stem cells waiting to be harvested.

It started slowly, as it always does. Tranquilizing my broken heart with the grace of your hand. ~~Caressing my face with love~~. Caressing my face with plans and knowledge and all the hope in the world to turn me into perfect; to transform me into perfection; to take the me out of me and place my carcass in a new body.

You show me pictures of my future that you've saved in your files. You, always the mad scientist thinking of new plans, of better homes, of crisper futures. Me, enamored, me, hammered, me melting and oozing, me with no body, no longer, me.

But I helped you cut. I opened my skin and let you turn it into a flag flapping in the air. You asked me: are you using this? I answered: it already belongs to you.

WATERLOG

First Steps

I am a ghost baby.

My fingers feel like air that is too icy. The kind that hurts your face when you walk through it. Sometimes when I get bored I will run my fingers up and down the legs of people who leave their legs exposed. They shiver, they seem so cold and then all of a sudden at peace. I think they deserve it, I never got to use mine.

On Tuesdays and Thursdays, I watch as my mother sits in class and thinks of things that are not me. I pretend sometimes that I will get up and climb into her backpack and finally go home with her. I dream of latching onto her breasts and feeding from the juice that was made while I waited inside of her. I can already feel the empty space entering me, sustaining me, helping me. Until I can move, I live off of water from people's shoes. The water that melts and stays after they walk in the snow or dry off from the rain. This water feels too liberating. It feels like the human part of me could swell up and fall out. I don't know what would happen to me if I was only ghost. I think I may float away. Perhaps if I was only ghost I would have died before I ever pretended I could live.

There are things that humans do that I can tell I never will. Mostly it has to do with feeling and objects. I can tell already that the only part of me that is not hollowed out is my mouth and my teeth. The only bones that bother to grow live in my useless mouth. All they do is sit around. Sometimes they chip on the ground when I drink the shoe water.

There are things that would be easier if I was only ghost. If I were just a ghost I wouldn't need to learn about these legs. Gravity would be something that I could forget about. I wouldn't have a need for tears. I wouldn't need to care about my mother — I am trying to cry for her attention, but my tears only fade away. They are more ghostly than I will ever be.

I am told from my observations that I will be able to walk within a year. I can crawl already, but my knees and my hands do not understand direction. I've decided that when I can walk I will follow my mother home. Before I am a year, I will meet my father.

FATHER

On the day that I find the legs and courage to walk into my mother's backpack, it is sunny outside. I think this is what tipped me off. I knew that if it were ever going to be the time, it was now. I felt like I could hear better, like I understood what happened in the world. On the many days I spent sleeping on this floor, nursing the water droplets from shoes, I dreamt of finally going home, of being released from this room. I stay in my mother's bag until we get into the car and then I follow what she does, I sit in the seat and try to buckle, but under my feeble hands I can't make it work. I figure I will be safe enough with her.

When we get home I look around at the place I will grow up in. There are two rooms with beds, one with water spots and one with heat spots. In the middle, there is a room filled with objects that my mother always sits on. I run around looking for my father, but I can't find him. I go into the water room and drink from the drips — this is where I meet him.

How did you get here, he asks me. I came with Mother, I tell him. Fuck, he says. I don't know what that means, I tell him. My teeth begin to chatter and he looks at them like they are the ghost and not me. How the fuck did you get those, he asks me. I was born with them, I tell him, do you think I'm ugly? My teeth chatter and clatter more and more. He sits next to me. No, he tells me. He apologies for his initial response and tells me that he loves me. Everything seems to be moving so fast now.

Father is nice to me from then on. He tells me that he loves me every day, but I just feel confused and say, you too. I'm not sure what love is, all I know is that I feel so small, so hollow. He is a tall man and almost reaches the ceiling. He tells me that Mother can't see us, that she doesn't know about us. He tells me I didn't have a chance at a mother and that he is to blame for that, he apologizes a lot. He tells me that my teeth are from my mother, that it is like they pulled each of hers to give to me. He tells me one day I will grow.

Father does not have a job, but that is because he is a ghost. We will live here until it no longer exists, he tells me. I am happy to have a home. I am happy to eat more than water off the floor. Father feeds me debris from the carpet while telling me the stories of how he and my mother met: It was fall, he said. That is when she moved in. I remember her walking up and down and up and down the stairs with more and more boxes. She was always something to look at. I didn't know how to approach her, not at first, but she actually made the first move. She would touch herself and moan whenever I was around and before I knew it we had made love. She got a bit distant after that, he tells me. Morning sickness and growing pains. She hasn't been the same since she had you.

MOTHER

Mother is self-absorbed, I think. She looks at herself in the mirror a lot and talks to herself like she could respond. This is a very different version of her than I saw in the classroom — there she was stiff and silent, always listening and thinking. Here she is movement, like a spaceship. And she is always doing something with her throat. Something like laughing or crying or coughing.

Mother lays on the couch on the days that she doesn't leave. She becomes the couch itself. She sleeps and eats and pees. She watches shows that I don't understand, but I laugh when she laughs so she thinks that I do. On the days when she doesn't leave I will lay next to her on the couch and pretend she can feel me. Sometimes I wrap myself around her and lay on her side as she lays on the couch. She always gets a blanket soon after, adding more layers between the two of us.

Mother is pretty and she doesn't know what to do with it. I hear her murmur in her room about how nothing fits her right and I never enter when I hear this — I know she wouldn't want me to hear her talking like this. Mother has hair that passes her shoulder and it is curly and beautiful and I think I could get lost in there if I wasn't paying attention. She wears bows and jewels in her hair sometimes and I think she looks like she is going to visit the president or royalty. Her eyes are a beautiful brown like a pile of mud on a rainy day — I want to lay down in it, make a mud pie and eat it.

Mother is pretty and I am left the ghost of her unwanted traits. My body is hollow and empty. My teeth are the only part of me that is straight. My hair is nonexistent, blending into my body, body blending into my arms, arms becoming legs. When I smile you can see the glimmer of my teeth — it is my best attribute. Mothers always give you the things you love most about yourself. Sometimes I pretend that Mother can see me and she paints me like she paints herself and tells me that I am as beautiful as she is.

I wish I could cry like Mother. During the week I see her well up and deflate, wiping and wiping and wiping her eyes. Her skin becoming wet, mossy like a tree after the rain. I want to catch them so I stand underneath her and open my mouth trying to catch as many as I can. They taste like a sweet salt, like dreams. I want to hug Mother, tell her that I am here, but she always puts a jacket on. I do not think she is trying to hurt me, but all I can think about is the distance she always needs from me. I love you Mother, I whisper in her ear. For a moment, she can almost hear me. I whisper back to myself, I love you too.

GIRLHOOD

I grow up without a mother, but this isn't her fault so I don't blame her. She couldn't see me, I was nothing to her. It wasn't that she didn't love me but rather that she couldn't have known to start. I am something like a suspicion, sneaking around her but never quite available.

I grow up without a mother, so I grow up with my father who is less pleasant. I don't think he expected a child, which is odd because he knew how sex works. He always gets defensive when I bring this up. I say, Dad, you did ask for me when you fucked that girl. He says, I didn't even know I had semen. Ghost semen is just as real as human semen, I tell him. It's not that you're a mistake, it's more like a misconception, he tells me — but that one goes right over my head.

I spend a lot of time watching my mother. I pretend that she knows I exist and is teaching me the things I need to know to be human. I talk to her as she does her hair, her makeup, as she gets dressed and runs out the door. I take notes in my ghost brain about how to apply eyeliner and curl my hair. I laugh when she tells me about what she did that weekend and pretend I know what it means to get *raw dogged* and *throw up Pink Whitney*. I always thought that was such a pretty name — Whitney. I tell my father to call me that, I say Mother threw me up just like she did Pink Whitney last weekend so that must be what she wanted to call me. Father laughs, either because I do not understand or because I finally do. Okay, Whitney, he tells me.

During my girlhood I think about women. I can tell when I look at myself that I am too small to be big, that I will have some growing to do. When Mother is gone I watch TV about what it means to come of age and what it means to blossom. I take notes on the things I will need to know when the blossoming comes: I will start to bleed uncontrollably, but not forever; boys will notice and that is okay because boys always have good intentions; my body will change and grow and become different than the hollow hole it is now, because I will have tits and hips and my see-through body will become less hollowed and more filled.

I ask my father what marriage is and if he and Mother are married. The TV says I need to wait until marriage to make a baby, I tell him. Not everyone does, he tells me, ghosts can't even get married so there is no point in waiting. I think a lot about how I am a bastard child, how God could never love me and now I will go to hell. I cry a lot for months and finally Father asks about it. I'm going to hell, I tell him. You're already dead, he says.

The Blossoming

It happens all at once. It is scary and painful and it feels for weeks like someone has stolen my body from within me.

I woke up at 3am one morning and was being torn apart. I screamed so loudly Mother and Father both woke up. It was as if this transcended out of me, like I couldn't be kept in this home anymore. My hair started to sprout out of my head in small tufts like grass. My body split into five different segments and out of those grew even more small small nodules. I ran into my mother's room to compare us. I had things to walk on like she did, now. I had things to grab with like she did now. My hair was much shorter, but it exists now.

In one movement, it felt like blood was coming out from my skin, like my see-through body was now a bubble filled with blood and puss. I wanted to pop it, I wanted to open the wound and bleed everywhere. I ran around the house knocking into doors and drawers and cabinets. I tried to find an edge sharp enough to burst my own bubble. Father pricked me with a pin and all of my insides seemed to come crashing down. He took me into the tub to bathe me.

Father held me in the tub as Mother showered, now unable to go back to bed. He wiped the blood from my face and told me this was the blossoming, that now I would be a woman. I'm not ready, I told him. You have no choice, he told me. I felt the water run over my body and for the first time it felt like I have movement, like I had any control. I separated my fingers and gnawed my teeth from pain. I looked down and saw lumps on my chest like Mother's. I'm scared, I told Father. Blood started pouring out from the lumps and Father told me that it was okay, that I would be okay, that blossoming is worse than birth, because you remember it.

At the end of my body, I saw it grow and grow and grow until I felt unstable. Legs, Father told me. You'll be as tall as me, he seemed to almost cry when he said this. I touched my face and could feel holes inside my head, my hands trembled. Don't worry, he told me, they will fill up soon — you're becoming just like your mother.

I wanted to cry. I wanted to stop being in between, I wanted to just have one. I had these appendages like humans, like my mother, but I was still hollow and empty, just a lousy ghost like my father. I don't want to be like her, I told my father. Almost as if she could hear us, my mother began to cry. I'm sorry, I whispered. I thought about what it would mean to be human, what it would be like to be like her. She is all talk, she is too solid and yet she is as fragile as glass. Father is fluid like water and all Mother does is cry and cry and excrete herself from herself. Human felt like hot metal skin and I did not want to be burned.

We sat in the shower, the three of us, a family, for about an hour. The water went from warm to cold and eventually Mother had to turn it off. Once it was off, we all sat like wet logs drying in the sun. Mother cried like she always did and Father rubbed my head like he always did.

I was the last to leave. I wanted to sit there by myself. Empty. I laid out in the tub and could fill it now. I stretched my limbs upwards and out and I tried to feel my body. Everything was numb. I could tell that I was now built like my mother, but the feelings of touch from my fingers never came. I thought about what Father said, how my mother would masturbate for him and I wondered if I had a vagina now. Another hole, like the ones on my face. No feelings, no lips or hair. It was all the same slick surface.

MOTHER

I think Mother can sense me now. There is a thickness around her that was never there before. I want to tell her I love her, that I've been watching for years, but she may not understand.

Mother looks more tired now, after the blossoming. She seems bogged down with regret, or maybe with birth. I wonder if her body could feel it too. It seemed like we were all feeling it. All of us in the tub in the shower, breathing together, mixing together. I wonder if Mother felt herself birth me again, as if all of her body parts were being taken and torn. I wonder if Mother felt the cloning of her body, like a machine stealing her and putting it into me. I wonder if Mother feels regret, now that I am entering a woman's existence. I wonder if she wanted a boy.

Mother looks emptier now that I am becoming more full. She is not a ghost, but she feels less human. I cannot see through her, but when I touch her hair in the morning it does not feel like it used to. It no longer feels like it could pull a boat across the ocean, but rather like it could drag her down to drown.

I think a lot about Mother dying. I hope she does not do it by water. The ghosts that are waterlogged never look right. You can't hear them well either. They always seem to be so busy, like they are searching for the right way to breathe on land again. The ghosts that drowned are always bloated and ugly, but it is not their fault. Water is an evil thing — why else would we weep it away? The ghosts who died in lakes and oceans, in seas and baths, they always seem the saddest, like they never had a chance.

I've thought of many futures for Mother and I wonder if any of them will come true. I think about what it would mean for her to grow old — would I grow alongside her? Would I continue to grow and then melt as she does? I've thought about the chances that she moves out and leaves us. I'm not sure what I would do then. How connected are mother and daughter? Will I disappear when she leaves? Will my body forget that it was ever partially human? I wonder if my father only loves me when my mother is around, like how people go crazy in front of cameras because then they will get attention. In some of the futures I imagine I turn human with my mother, like another blossoming, but real. One day I emerge from the ghost world into the human one and then she can love me in a real way. I would tell her about Father and about what it means to be a mother even when you don't know. My favorite future is the one when she joins us, she dies and then we are all ghosts. My teeth fall out, but it is okay, because I have Mother and Father and me.

FATHER

Father doesn't know how to look at me after the blossoming. It is the case with many fathers and daughters once they become human. It is as if the world was fake and happy until girls grow breasts and legs and become real.

Father still loves me, but there is not much to do in the realm of ghosts, because there is so much boredom. It is as if time has stopped, but we are forced to think it keeps going. I see him watch her. He gazes at Mother and thinks about how he didn't know what he was doing. I can tell by the way he looks at her that he loves her deeply and truly. Sometimes I wonder if he ever made me a sibling. I think about them being dumber than me, maybe they never found their way out of the classroom, they never learned how to crawl or walk or slurp up the shoe water from the floor.

Mother brought someone home once. He was tall, not quite as tall as Father, and he seemed kind. I watched and thought about the fact that they could create a baby that was real, a baby that they both saw and felt and knew. I think they may have tried, but it never took. I watched Father that night as he debated and thought about checking in on her, knowing he wouldn't like what he saw.

Father is lonely, he seems more lonely now than ever. I think when I was younger he thought of me as a friend, an ally, a partner in a lonely ghost world. Now that I have grown I think about leaving. He cannot. He is doomed to be here forever, to live here and only here. But I wasn't born in this house and I have legs and arms and breasts and those can take me anywhere. I told him that I would not go. I promised him. But he tells me that it isn't fair, that I should travel like he did in the time when he was alive. I ask him about it — when he was alive — he tells me that it was wonderful, because he could taste peaches and pears. He tells me that he could make love and make music and that he even thought about being on TV and he wishes that he had because then I could have seen who he used to be. I tell him that I don't care about who he used to be because I know who he is now and now he is my father. He tells me I am like my mother and I smile. I smile, but I wonder how much he even knows her.

ADULTHOOD

When I woke up today my mother was dead. She died at night, in her sleep, or maybe before then. It was as if I looked away and suddenly she was limp and sad. I waited for her, for her ghost to come into my eyes, to be able to see her and meet her and feel what it meant to have a mother, to be a child of parents.

But she never came.

I went to her body to ask her when she was coming and that was when I reached my own adulthood. That was when daughter became mother and ghost baby became human woman. The ways in which the blossoming stretched and bled is the opposite of what it felt like to become her, to step into the body of my own mother. It was like exiting a door and entering the outside air in the spring — it is relaxing and calm. It is peace.

In my human body I can feel what it means to have skin. I can sense that there are organs within me, they have filled my hollowness, they have reduced my vacancy. I take my clothes off and see what it means to not be see-through, rather I take shape and fill the mirror. I start the shower and I can feel water, but it is not like the water I lapped off the floor. This water is like love, like the touch of my father when I am lost.

I look over to him, my father sitting there watching. Thank you, I tell him. My mother answers, next to him, by his side. She tells me, you're welcome. They sit, finally together, finally in love like my father always knew. They sit, holding each other as much as vacancy can.

TO TEND TO

A Lust Story

The setting is a bar that you can imagine. The characters are those of the normal people that come to this bar but also you. The plot is that of the stories you may have heard before: you meet a person of the sexual identity you prefer and you dance around a little, or maybe do karaoke, or maybe just sit and talk and you feel like your knees are weak. But in this version these knees being weak are not a good thing, because they couldn't keep their respective genitals in their pants and they take you home and you wake up confused and later you go to a lot of therapy and finally feel like you could be okay again sometime soon.

An alternative ending: consent. That is the better ending, but in reality sometimes the ending is not the better ending.

Another ending: you end up dead on the couch of a serial killer.

A possible ending: a wedding in which you are happy, because this ending comes after the consent.

The moral of the story: sex is okay when there is consent.

(Even, and perhaps especially, before marriage.)

A Series of Diagrams:
Ranking Tactics of Childhood Bullies

Fig. 1

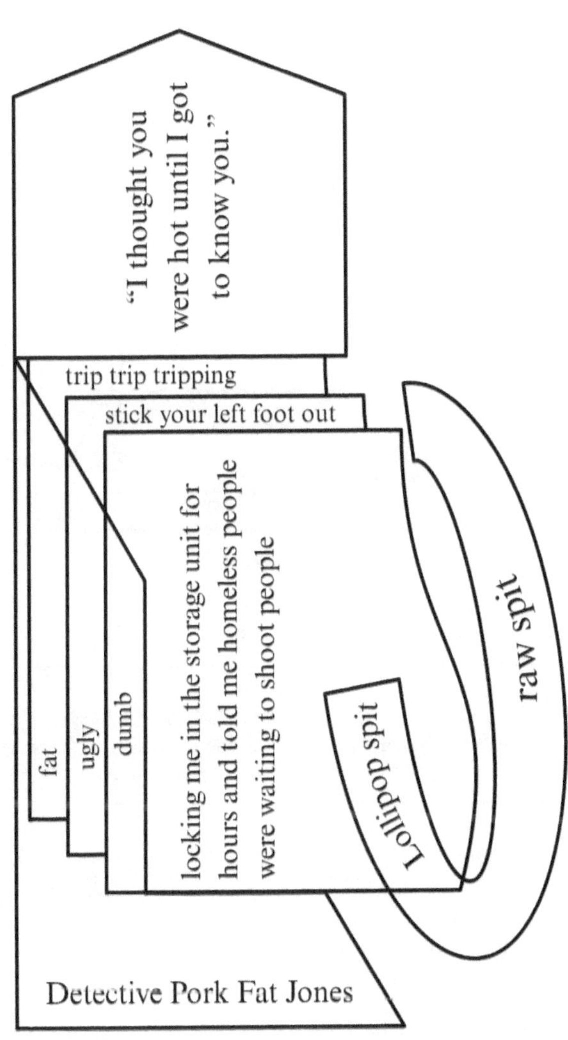

A Series of Diagrams:
Ranking Tactics of Childhood Bullies

Fig. 2

Key:

★ Detective Pork Fat Jones

◎ Stealing My Shoes and Throwing Them Into Traffic

〰 You Were Hot Until I Got To Know You

◆ Stealing My Crutches So I Couldn't Walk

••• Locking Me In Storage Unit

A Series of Diagrams:
Ranking Tactics of Childhood Bullies

Fig. 3

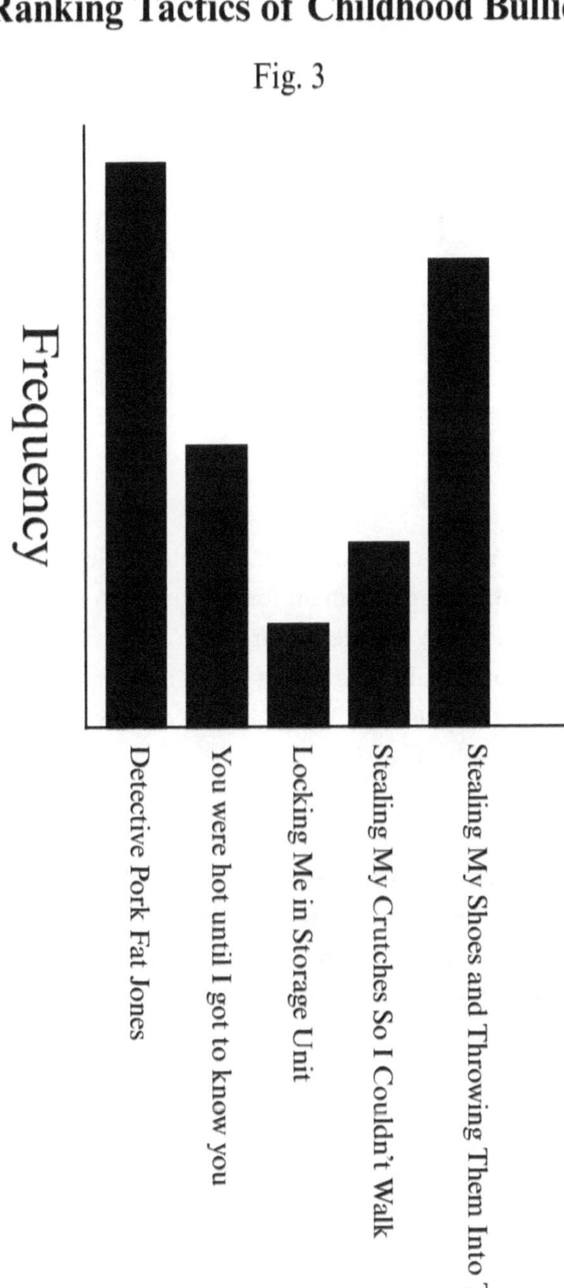

You Hold Me Down

I'm fourteen. You're six years older. A welder. The singer in my brother's band. The replacement for the guy who knew when to move on. Who was younger than you. You're always staying longer than you should. The rest of the band hangs around high school waiting to graduate. You're legally allowed to drink. You buy the drinks.

You're always around. I'm always enamored. Always wanting to grow up faster. Always thinking I need to change. What should I change? Anything. Hair. Outfits. Maybe swap my skin and bones with a friend. I just want to feel different than before. Let me change into a [woman]. Aren't I already? The world tells me I'm ready to be a [woman]. And I want to, want to listen. I can be your [woman], can't I? Please?

You drive your car with your tattoos and your piercings. When you sing you have a loudness like you aren't worried who hears you. Always wanting to be watched. Always watching. With your beautiful blue eyes. I melt into them. Trapped in them. Trap me.

I'm in your bedroom. You tell me: *We don't have to do anything you're not comfortable with. Like I know we've texted but obviously I wouldn't hold you to any of that. I mean have you ever even been spanked? 'Cause if you haven't then maybe we don't want to go all the way today like maybe I could just show you how I like to worship feet? I don't know. Whatever you feel comfortable with. Like maybe we should just kiss and see where it goes?*

You drop me off at high school after so I can see a basketball game with my friends. You remind me not to tell anyone. *You can trust me,* I say. I beg to you in my mind: *Please trust me. I need something to remind me that someone out there wants me to continue. And if you trust me then maybe I can trust myself. So please please please trust me.*

You did. We spend years hidden in cars or in your room at your parents' house.

I'm naked in your room. You're naked on the floor. You ask me: *Have you ever stomped someone's balls before? It really isn't that hard. Don't worry, I like the pain. If you go too hard I will tell you. So feel free to ram your fucking heel into my balls and don't forget to tell me that I have a small, small, tiny fucking penis and that I don't deserve to not be in pain. Just like really fucking go to town on my balls and my penis and even laugh at it. Just have a good time like all high schoolers want to do. Just be mean to me.*

I'm sixteen. You're still six years older. You tell me that when I am seventeen we can take this public. That when I'm seventeen the age difference won't matter. As if when I turn seventeen you will stop aging. That you will no longer be six years older.

I'm eagerly waiting for one more year. We've already made it this far so in one more year I will finally be a [woman]. And I cannot wait to be your [woman]. I cannot wait to offer myself up to you publicly.

Until then. I watch porn trying to understand what it is that [women] do. How it is that I could please you. It's hard being the younger one because how do I keep your attention when I am so afraid that you will find someone who can do it better. Who has done it before. Who can do it do it do it. So I watch porn and you show me porn and I try to be the porn that you want me to be. I try to be what you want. I go to sex shops to get the sex toys you want and the bondage supplies you say we need. And I watch all the porn on how to squeeze the life out of your balls until you cry like a bitch.

We go on dates far away. You take me out to dinner. But no, I can't get that. And I will say *Yes sir, whatever you say* because you must be right. Who am but a [little girl].

On dates you let the secret secrete out. I am not your first. There was a young girl before me. A friend of your sister's when you were younger. I'm full of jealousy. I dye myself green. All my belongings green. All my body hair green. All I eat green. I want to be your first. Your only. Why would you choose someone before me?

You're not the only one of my brother's friends I have thought about fucking. You are just the one I thought about most. Wanted the most. Craved craved craved. But other friends of yours, at your age, tell me of their fetishes. Like *Duh, what sixteen-year-old wouldn't want to know that you're into period blood?* You high-five your friend as you make jokes of taking me to Paris. Of making me into the Eiffel Tower. I laugh laugh laugh because I do not understand. I'm Googling, never understanding. I research research research to become [any object you want me to be].

I'm crying, always crying. You're crying, always pouting. You tell me that if only I understood what it was like to really feel things, maybe then I would understand. You tell me to stop sending pictures of me cutting myself open, that I'm not a doctor. But I want you to see through me. To see through me to my illnesses. But you're always putting on blinders.

I'm seventeen. You're somehow still six years older. You did not lie though, and for that I give you credit. We're lovers. We're in love. We're public as fuck. You're not afraid to tell the world that you want to date a seventeen-year-old because technically it isn't illegal — you've looked into it. Plus, isn't seventeen basically eighteen?

You bring me to a work event where I'm the youngest one. No one asks my age. If I had to guess, I am the only one in high school. The only one who needs a parent's signature for forms. The only one not paying rent. The only one applying to colleges. The only one.

You take me home to meet your parents. And your siblings. Your sister is in my grade. Your brother, younger than my youngest sister. We eat tacos. They ask me about what I will study in college and offer me advice on how to take trains to and from so I can get more work done.

I'm going to college. You're staying home. I'm moving hours and hours away. We've discussed how hard it will be to stomp on your balls from hours away. So we decide to have an open relationship. We discuss the hardship of long distance; if should we be engaged; how we will be fine if we stay open because we won't be bogged down with all of our horniness and how that's that hardest thing to contend with after all; how I really do agree that we should be open because I waited long enough for this relationship to be real; how I will not continue to wait to make out with all my friends or get drunk and get laid; how this is one of the only things we truly agreed on.

You're visiting. All my friends thinking: *Wow, he is older. He can get us drinks. But also don't you find him to be a bit immature or don't you think he's a bit old for us?* You're the only one blacked out on our college campus. You're drinking drinking drinking. You're full of confidence that you can check out all the hot hot hot of-age girls and no one will bat an eye. You're in your hunting grounds.

I'm home for break. You're driving me around. I'm nervous about how I look so I ask: *Do you think I'm hotter now or in high school?* You answer: *Oh, high school.* I cry and cry and you don't understand but I just cry cry cry.

I'm away at school with friends. I study English and Political Science. I write papers and I read and I take the required classes and I also write write write my silly little words. You give me a story for Valentine's Day that you wrote just for me, I attempt to workshop it, you shut down and tell me I don't get it. You leave and my life continues.

It's during this time that I remember too vividly that I am not your first. Another girl in my grade, another girl who knew your sister, another girl years before me that you picked up and talked to and I don't know the specifics besides you got in a fight and she left your car in traffic. That, and I know your sister wouldn't talk to you for years after. Echoing the sentiment she yelled at us when we showered together in your mom's apartment when we thought no one would be home. Us hiding behind the curtain as she yelled and screamed: *You ruin everything.* She didn't know who was in there with you, but I wonder if somewhere inside she has considered this pattern: *It's never just one young girl.*

I'm eighteen and home for the summer. You're somehow wearing this six-year difference for the first time. "Hold Me Down" by Motion City Soundtrack playing in my mind as I go over to talk to you. You ask: *Shouldn't we fuck first?* I answer: *No, because I don't think I want to stay in this relationship because I have more fun when I am not with you.* You say: *This is why we should have fucked first.* You were the one on the ground. You were the one below me. You were the ones with the balls being crushed. But you were the one holding me down. You were the one preventing me from [blossoming]. You were the one that didn't want me to [bloom].

You tell everyone it's mutual but my brother knows it is not, therefore everyone knows you got your heart broken by a [girl] six years younger. You tell me you think you will still end up with me. We are both dating other people. I tell you no it won't happen. I wonder who stomps your balls now, I wonder if they found you on your sexy Facebook where you send unsolicited lingerie pictures, I wonder if your parents somehow knew and that is why your name rhymes with pedophile.

I'm twenty-five. I'm unsure of how to engage with you now. I'm unsure how to internalize this relationship. How something that always felt consensual is now tainted with grooming and statutory rape. I'm watching from afar. I'm a married woman. I'm no longer thinking of you with daisies and roses. I'm thinking and I'm internalizing. I'm traumatized.

A LOVE STORY

This is a love story about a girl who loved herself so much she went to school and got an education and with that education she got more education until she felt like she was happy with the formal education she got so she learned and learned and learned on her own when she wanted to and she worried about nothing but herself.

Bagel Baby

Bagel Baby was not a baby of bagels but a really big bagel advocate. She ate bagels mostly every day except for the days in which she didn't. She loved them because they held a lot of hope and dreams, except for the vacant middle that made her feel at home.

The story of Bagel Baby is a happy one, because she continues to eat bagels throughout all of it. She even started renaming the other things she loved Bagel. When she gave birth at twenty-three, she named the baby Bagel and now that baby is a bagel baby, the baby of Bagel Baby. She loves Bagel and will not eat her. She will die never knowing the taste of the bagel she birthed. Bagel goes by Bagel. She is proud of her mother.

This is now the story of Bagel, the baby of Bagel Baby who truly feels indifferent towards most bagels. Sometimes the loves of our parents are not gifted down to us. Sometimes we have to find the things we love independent of the things thrust upon us. On the anniversary of Bagel Baby's death, Bagel eats a plain bagel with cream cheese, her mother's favorite. She eats about twenty of them in the day and goes to bed full and happy, feeling closer to her mother.

Bagel is a girl of many wants and few needs, I guess that is like most of us. She wants to make the world a better place, but she needs to pay rent. So she goes to work at the accounting firm that was willing to hire a girl named Bagel. Bagel thinks often of the ways in which she wishes she could meet a partner that could also get past the bagel of her. Bagel looks like the embodiment of a cinnamon raisin bagel, a true beauty.

If her mom could have picked a boy for her it would have been a coffee man that smelled like ground beans in the morning and felt like cream and sugar in her mouth. She did not know however that Bagel was less into coffee and more into tea, which is to say that coffee is not her type, which is to say that Bagel is a lesbian. If Bagel could pick the dream partner, it would be the type of tea that smelled like pumpkin, the type of tea she could dunk her cinnamon raisin body into.

At her work as an accountant, there is a religious lady who often asks people to come to church with her. She hands out pamphlets and flyers that explain why it could be fun. Bagel does not want to go, but one Sunday she wakes up at 6am and decides she has nothing better to do. When she goes to church she is not moved by The Lord, but she is moved by the religious lady's voice that feels like a sweet sweet scent in her ears. After the pews are emptied, she waits around and tells her how much she loved her voice, *It felt like sweetness in my ears.* "Thank you, Bagel." For some reason, Bagel cannot remember the name of the lady and she starts to feel embarrassed. "Do you want to go out for coffee?" *Oh, yes, you.*

They decide to walk across the street to a coffee shop that is surprisingly empty. *Where are all the religious people?* She laughed,

"They don't really come here, they usually go for a real sit down spot." *Oh, I'm sorry.* "Don't be, I wanted to come here with you." Bagel's heart starts fluttering and she feels so happy that she orders a plain bagel with cream cheese. The religious lady orders the same. *It was my mom's favorite.* "It's my favorite too." *Maybe you're my mother reincarnated.* Bagel feels like maybe that's offensive, *Oh, I'm sorry. Is that offensive? I mean, I don't know how God works.* "Honestly, me either. All I know is that my parents liked it so I just always go back." *Are you not Religious?* "No, I'm Judy."

At work Bagel feels like she's in love now. She thinks about the way that Judy is sweeter than a pumpkin tea — she's sweet like a pumpkin pie. Her skin is soft and silky. Bagel thinks about the way she would taste and dreams of eating her. On Thursday Judy brings Bagel a plain bagel with cream cheese. Bagel dreams of their wedding where all they will serve is bagels and pumpkin pie.

Bagel asks Judy to the grocery store and then to her house. Judy says yes, she would love to. At the grocery store they buy chicken and broccoli and bread and even bagels *for the morning.* That night after dinner, they were full and happy. They play board games and after long enough Judy hollows out Bagel's insides like she's on a diet and she eats them until Judy is full and full and Bagel is complete. In the morning they eat the bagels — onion with butter.

Bagel and Judy date for a while, they spend many mornings trying different bagels like salt and rye and pumpernickel and at one point a Buffalo bagel. Bagel loves the way in which Judy never says no to another bagel, this lets Bagel know she will never be a disappointment.

There is a moment in the future where Bagel and Judy will have a baby. They hired someone to give Bagel their sperm and Judy fucked her with it. Bagel and Judy will spend nine months waiting for their baby and a week before the baby is born, Judy will die. Bagel will be crushed and sad and never the same. Bagel will name their daughter Pumpkin. Pumpkin will always be sweet and honey to Bagel, Pumpkin will always be the light of Bagel's life because she knows that is what Judy would have wanted.

In the present. Judy and Bagel are just getting engaged. Judy is the one to propose and they will have their wedding at the church that makes Judy feel closer to her parents and they serve bagels and pumpkin pie. The guests are disappointed but understanding. In their vows Judy tells Bagel that she loves her and Bagel says the same thing. They spend the whole day holding hands and they feel no need to say hi to their guests, rather they feed each other the bagels and pumpkin pie. This will always be their favorite memory.

ACORNS

I carry my ghost around like a parrot on my shoulder. He whines and chirps and tells me stories of people I will never meet. *Barney and Carla went to the beach every summer, but they never invited me.* I roll my eyes, always out of view; the ghost always on my shoulder, unwilling to shift spots or take notice of where he is sitting. *I voted for Nixon, okay? No one told me I had to, but I did.* My eyes never able to stare, never able to rest comfortably on what he looks like, never able to transfix. *I was homeless for a month in the early seventies. My mom kicked me out, my sister never answered me, my dad was already dead.*

I wonder where his dad went. I wonder if I was cursed to carry this ghost on my shoulder; I wonder if he was cursed to sit with me. His dad must have done something right for him to be off in the space untethered to a girl, sitting.

When I try to fall asleep, I close my eyes and picture the days I did not carry ghosts: childhood filled with flowers, teenage years filled with flowers, my early twenties filled with trees and rocks. Twenty-three and I feel something hit my chest. I wipe and wipe and wipe until I realize there is nothing on me. Under a tree, filled with loneliness, a ghost fell on my lap. He crawled onto my shoulder and now when I am on the brink of sleep he says, *Barney never told Carla how we met. She always assumed it was church or school, but Barney and I met on jet skis.* He never hears me when I ask him not to talk, when I tell him I'm trying to sleep. *You sound like my mom but you can't kick me out. We met on **jet skis**. Do you not understand?* I tell him again and again that I do understand and if he waits until morning then I might even care. *I was homeless, on a jet ski, and he took me in.* I stop responding.

I quit my job to take care of my ghost. He is a full-time job. Worse than a baby: he can talk. Worse than a child: he can't move away. I envy his mother every day, some escape to this whining as he perches on my shoulder. I am on disability, the curve of my neck and back never the same after I start lugging around the body of this ghost on my shoulder. *Are you lazy?* NO, I shout, but the world seems to turn to look at me; my empty apartment judging my volume. *It was **just a question**. You never ask me any questions anymore.* I've been busy, I tell him. I'm sorry, I say again and again, but I never expected to be a mother to a middle-aged ghost. *Middle-aged!? MIDDLE-aged??* The silent treatment is a treat.

My parents call me every Thursday and I tell him he needs to be quiet. He doesn't like how I talk to him. I tell him that he can go and sit somewhere else if he doesn't like it, but he seems to almost cry at this. He is so lonely his body shudders at the thought of unclimbing, of dismounting, of undoing. *I'm sorry*, he whispers in my ear. Faint. Passing.

I call my parents every Thursday and after every phone call, I hear from my ghostly parrot of a man that I should be more thankful for them. They offer to send me money and he urges me to accept. *Imagine what you could do with that. Maybe we could jet ski.* I tell him again that I cannot swim. That I do not wish to take him to the beach. The lake? I ask him again and again. *No, no, no, no.* We never seem to leave the apartment anymore.

I try to catch a glimpse of him in the mirror and on occasion I do. When he is lazy and forgets I can see his reflection if he does not try to hide it, I observe him. I brush my teeth on a timer, two minutes of observation at best. Often this is crumbled into seconds of repetition. Gray hair, half the teeth, wrinkles and wrinkles and wrinkles. He is always touching my hair as if I am the pet he has come to love, as if he is not the ghost that landed on my lap. He looks at me as if he is there to save me, as if I am the adopted. When he catches me staring, he disappears.

I love you. He only says this when he thinks I am asleep. He only says this at his loneliest. He only thinks about it when I refuse to go to the jet skis. *I love you very much, thank you.* I know that he cannot sleep but he turns into a hum as my mind fades into dreams.

And I dream: about the ways in which I can't see my parents. That I don't want to see them with my ghost on my shoulder. You can't explain the intricacies of childhood, of family hierarchy, of losing yourself when you go home, to a ghost that has only been here three years. I dream: of going back to the lake with them. Of cuddling next to my mother while my father stokes the fire. I dream: of returning to the life of a child, rather than the beginnings of adulthood.

And sometimes he helps me: I dream of: him as a child. Playing in the sand. Building castle after castle at the beach. I dream of: the month he slept on benches and couches and one time on the street. Lately he makes me dream of: the jet skis.

When I went back to work I used my first paycheck to buy Barney his own jet ski. Carla didn't live with us yet. She was nothing but a nobody then. I think of what I would use my paychecks for if I lived back at home. I think about the gardening equipment I would buy for the garden I could have if I wasn't stuck in the only apartment I could afford. I think of the hammock I would plant between the trees in my parents' yard if I could move closer and live near them. I do not think of what my ghost would want.

And yet, he always asks me, *Do you think you could buy me a gift? My birthday is coming up this month and I know you haven't been able to the past couple of years.* I feel tears well behind my eyes, I feel them bubble in my ears. I want nothing more than to live my own life again. Why does he think I want to reward him? *I don't need my own jet ski, I obviously couldn't ride it. But maybe we could go to the ocean and see how much a ride is.*

I've taken to ignoring him. The closer his birthday gets, the louder he becomes. *Barney would have loved this.* I yell at him for the first time, Then go see Barney! *I can't, he's dead.* The whines of ghost tears fill my ears. So are you, I tell him. And I say it again and again, you are dead, you're dead, I don't know who you are or why you voted for Nixon, but you're just as dead as Barney. *I can't be as dead as Barney! He is lost at the bottom and I died at the top. No one is as dead as Barney.*

I tell myself I could go to an exorcist or to a church and sometimes I drive to the parking lots. *I went to church with my sister and my mom after Dad left. I drove them.* Everything has to be a story. With the ghost on my shoulder, I cannot escape storytime. *He left us and left this world. Such a quitter, always quitting. Mom always missed him.*

I drive to things I think are new, but he always seems to do his research. He knows every fast food chain, every small town diner in the area. I don't believe he stays with me while I sleep, but every time I wake up I feel the weight of sleeping with a ghost.

I tell myself that he isn't looking and I start to Google dead Barneys in the area. He yells at me that I won't find him. That I can't find *his* Barney because *his* Barney was never found. And he's right. There are no Barneys at the bottom of the ocean. He whines and whines and I feel him tap my shoulder as if tears could fall from his face. How old was he, I ask. *My age, months earlier.* He hides in plain sight. I can feel his body weight but I cannot see his ghostly apparition in the corner of my eye. He never does this when we're not in front of a mirror. I'm sorry, I whisper.

Thursdays become contentious. My parents tell me they are going to come visit. They haven't seen me in years and they miss me. I tell them they can come once I am feeling better. They always reassure me that it may never happen. *You'll feel better one day,* he tells me. I've been starting to understand that he believes it. I can know now that he doesn't understand this is his fault. *One day you'll feel better.* I can feel him caress my head. I consider telling him I love him.

My groceries are always delivered and I almost always eat the same things. Breakfast: yogurt and fruit. Lunch: sandwich, chips, salad. Dinner: tacos or pasta or sleep. *You need more meat in your diet. A nice steak might fix you.* I buy two and make them both for us. His sits out for days, slowly molding. Mine is eaten in twenty minutes. I cannot get the courage to tell him I didn't like it.

Barney and Carla met at church. Carla always thought I'd end up like my dad, but the only person I ever had was Barney. Mom, she needed space. Sister, she needed Mom. Me and Barney? We needed our jet skis. He talks over the TV now. Restless from the death he's been forced into. Agonized by the need to stand on a girl's shoulders. *Barney knew everything. Everything. If there was some-*

thing I didn't know, I went to Barney. If there was something I needed, I went to Barney. Carla never liked me all that much. He laughs, chuckles, sighs. *Carla was almost perfect for Barney. If she just didn't make him give up the water.*

Barney never did, though. That's all I ever take away from him. Barney couldn't give it up just like he couldn't give up his best friend, my ghost, my closest friend.

I dream of jet skis on my own. No vision of the wrinkly man who sits with me day in and day out. I have no desire to learn to swim. I have no desire to go to the beach. But at night I dream of what his life would have felt like. What it means to be with Barney. I know now why he tells me he loves me.

What were you doing in that tree? I ask him. *I just missed Barney.* You said he was underneath, I remind him. *He is. He always will be. But I was too scared of jet skis after him, I wouldn't go alone. I thought we'd all go to the same spot, but your other shoulder is so empty.* I didn't ask for this, you know? *And you think I did?*

I found you at the tree you hanged yourself at. You dropped into my lap like an acorn wanting to regrow, rebirth, reanimate. You made a home on my shoulder, on my body, of my body. You are my ghost I carry around, I touch my shoulder to hold your hand.

TO SPILL OVER

Love at First Sight(s)

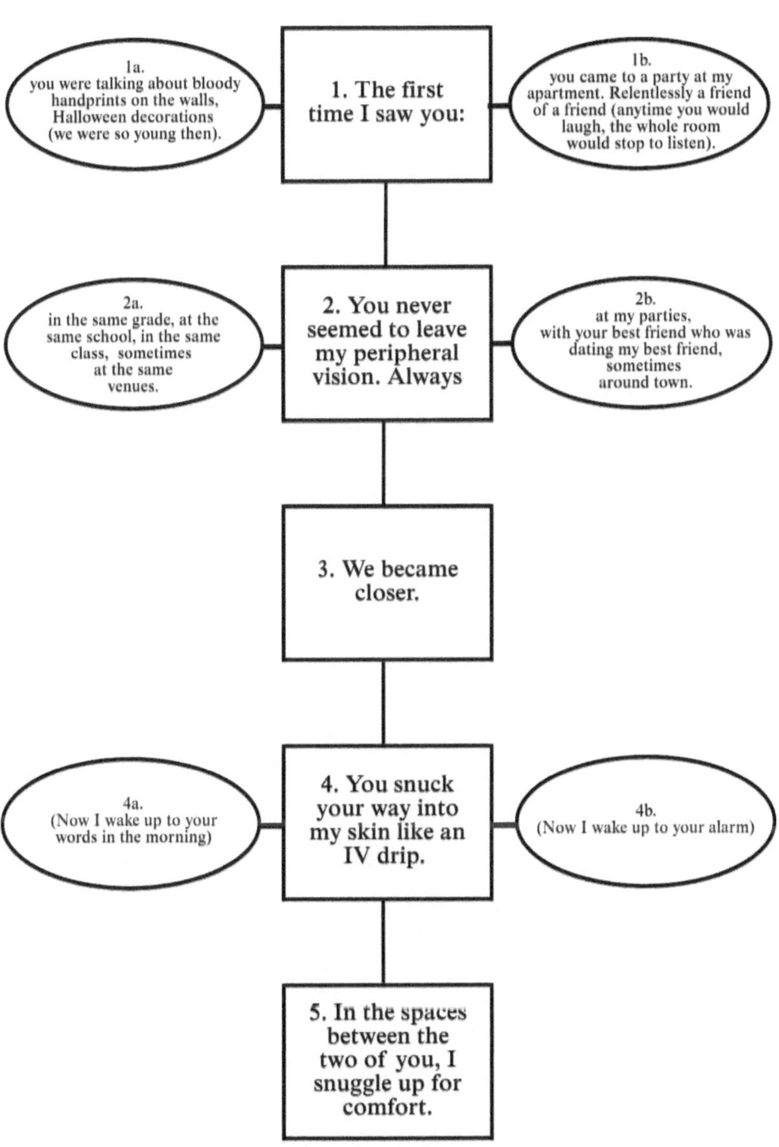

BOLIDES

Stars hung like bodies on chains and we all watched as some of the bodies swung, fell and disappeared. "That was a big one." He stated it like he stated most things: with the type of confidence you can't fit inside your pocket. "Bolides."

The three of us held hands as we walked to the dock. We held hands like kids hold ice cream cones: we held them like all our joy would die if we lost it, if I happened to let go I knew I would cry and cry and cry until someone gave me another hand to hold. We all held hands as the night sky seemed to warn us of something.

"It's Friday the 13th." They said it as if they were conjuring the haunting themselves. I shivered with fear because I always knew better, my mother raised me better than to walk around at night, especially on a Friday the 13th. "We're going to cut through the graveyard." They said and we did. They said and they released my hand. I clung on to him, I refused to let go of him. *I'm supposed to be the spooky one*, I thought as our feet touched soil. *I'm supposed to like walking in graveyards at night.* I wanted to, I wanted to, but all I could picture was the people I'd be waking up. A graveyard no longer accepts new graves, it is just a row of dead people. Rows and rows and underneath the graves are smaller columns of people stacked on top of one another. There is no room under a graveyard, there are only more graves.

I felt I could breathe again after we finally made our way through the dead bodies. I felt finally like I was a balloon floating away. It was thanks to him, to his hand, to the way in which he grasped my fingers that made my heart float away. That was the first time I fell in love with him. Holding hands under the moon-light, me and him. They are standing right next to us — they are not ruining the moment, this moment was meant for three, it was meant for me and him falling in love and them standing with us observing this love, heightening this love, making this love real in the world we're standing in. (There are other times and moments that the three of us make up. Most of these moments are times in the past, times when I never knew if either of you actually liked me or if it was all pity all along. Moments on the computer where we judge each other with sincerity and permission. Moments where we are huddled together in laughter. I will always hear both of your laughs in moments of the dark.)

When we made it to the dock, the sky seemed to light up — not to become day but rather a less haunting night. It lit up in the way that said *Congratulations, you made it to your destination. You now have more time to enjoy not dying.* We made it to the dock and we lay with our feet in the water and both of you in my hands. "Do we just keep holding hands?" Someone asked. (You can never pinpoint a voice in the darkness.) We all laughed, we laughed the kinds of laughs you can laugh when it is dark and you do not see any other bodies. We all laughed and they let go of my hand right away. He lingered. He lingered with me, waiting a moment before we released. Enjoying the way in which we felt in each other's hand. He lingered and I lingered and our love lingered between us, resting on the dock.

(We released our hands and the world felt darker. Not much. But some. We released and I remembered what life feels like outside of warmth and outside of support. I became a baby, only for a moment, a baby who couldn't hold its head up. I was flailing. For a moment.)

"There is phosphorescence in the water," they said. On cue, we all sat up, dangled our legs, and splashed the water until we could see the creatures illuminate. "It's so pretty." We all said it but all in different ways. We all meant it in all the ways one could say it.

"Sharks feed at night." I said. Every time a wave felt rushed or something made a sound in the water, I could feel eyes on me, I could tell they were all sharks. I took my legs out of the water. I sat criss-cross applesauce on the dock as you both fearlessly dangled into shark-infested waters. I was in awe, I am in awe. *I'm supposed to be the spooky one*, I thought, *but I won't be the one eaten by a shark.*

There was a moment when a car came. It seemed as though they might drive onto the dock, through us, and into the ocean. Of course they just stopped at the edge. They saw the look on my face, "They're probably just watching the sky like us." "They could be murderers." I said it, of course I said it. "They're more likely drug dealers. Some people put drugs in lobster traps and they come at night to collect them." They thought this would soothe me. He knew it wouldn't. I felt then, when he grabbed my hand, like I could float under the water with him. Like if I had to choose between facing drug dealers or sharks that I could talk myself into the water *with him*. (Without him, without his hand, I would likely shrivel up into fear.) I thought of what it meant to continue laying there after the sharks and the drug dealers. I wondered how foolish we were to leave our backs to them. I looked up at the stars but I felt my body tighten with worry that at any moment an axe could blow through my head. It would be me first, then him, then them. Unless they were the ones to orchestrate all of this. Then it would be me, then him, then release for them.

What would it mean to never return? If we never left the dock. If we never walked back home, wet bodies after jumping in (only he could convince me), feet on the gravel, soaking up the pain. What would it mean to own the dock? To never leave, to refuse the drug dealers, to tell them that we won't tell, that we do not care, but we cannot leave this place of love. In the moment, I never knew if love could exist anywhere else. If I fell in love on the dock, could love persist anywhere else? I am oozy with love for both of you. My body will not stop creating and secreting more and more love for you both. My house reeks with the smell of love.

We laid, the three of us. We laid and watched the stars. I laid next to the two of you. Me in the middle. Monkey in the middle, but he did not keep the jokes away from me, he would pass the ball my way. Them, me, him. We laid and watched the stars as they tried to keep existing. So many would pass by us, a parade of shooting stars just waiting to be wished upon. Those were ours. I know that somewhere in the world someone else could have seen our stars and made wishes too, but I know those stars weren't listening to them. Those stars were created for us, for the three of us. Those stars were made so we could whisper to them, tell them our secrets and dreams. Most importantly, those stars were there for us to fall in love. We told them our wishes and they enacted their own. Now when I see stars dangle, I think of falling in love with him.

DEBRIS DESIRE

I always knew it was possible for me. I knew the whole time that my love does not end, it is a well with no bottom, I can put all of me into more than one. I always knew I could handle it, but I never knew if it would happen. I never knew two of you could exist in such perfect forms that you both take my breath away: I am wheezing and gasping and dying to know all of you.

There is an overlap in timelines, but it is not a perfect circle. We all know that time is a construct. We all know that at the bottom of the ocean there are piles of love, mounds of debris and desire, at the bottom of the sea are anchors made of hearts. We all know how to find the myth of endless love, we will all be piles of skins that were just trying to sew ourselves together, stitch love into time so we could finally be long enough to reach the bottom, finally long enough to join the debris.

If time is cyclical, if I have to keep living this timeline again and again: I couldn't imagine it without either of you, I don't think I could untie my boat from your dock.

NOBODIES

Nobody gets me like my husband. No one understands the ways in which punk music can change how your mind absorbs new information. No one gets the way that you can do your own thing and be by yourself and show so much love in solitude.

But nobody gets me like my boyfriend. No one understands gentle like them. No one gets that your hands are not weapons but vessels of love that you can form into extensions of your deepest soul; your touch is love emulsified.

Still, nobody gets me like my sister. Growing up girls without moms and moms to each other. No one gets that you can stand your ground and not be polite, that not everything needs to be done with nice, sometimes things just need to be done.

And nobody gets me like my brother. Shoving each other into people in pits and knocking the hardcore dancers into a real circle. No one gets that sometimes things need force and action and that is always someone's job.

So nobody gets me like my dad. Raising me from a child, throwing me when I throw up on him for the first time, wiping my ass when I can't hold my alcohol. No one gets that love is continuous and never-ending and always to be done.

And it reminds me of my husband, nobody gets me like him. The way he slows down time to explain the logic in every decision. How he has unpacked the pros and the cons, and also there is this new album that I would love. I always always do.

The music plays and I know that nobody gets me like my boyfriend. The lyrics they analyze and we could talk about it for hours. The stories we tell again and again and the games we play to unpack our lives together. They show me their heart and I kiss it on the nose.

Which is how I always said goodbye to my sister in high school. And nobody gets me like her. The way that we can finish the thoughts in each other's mind. The unspoken language of sisterhood, how she can always call at just the right moment.

And my brother is calling now. Nobody gets me like him. Nobody understands the way in which horror unravels the time we spend on this earth. The ways in which horrific fiction can heal the wounds of our horrific lives. He sends me his recommendations and I watch them all.

Like my dad still watches over us. Nobody gets me like my dad. Like the person who is a part of me and also still alive. Our minds bowls of spaghetti, ever swirling. We can talk on the phone for hours and when it is time to go, more and more hours pass.

170

And still.

MY STICKY SWEET(S)

So how do you fall in love again when you've already done it once? How do you etch someone into the glasses you've already carved? It always just seems to appear. I have love oozing out of my fingertips, sappy and sugary, I let it rub off on the people I care about; I douse my friends with my sticky sweet — it just so happens you couldn't escape, it just so happens you were leaking too, it just so happens that we are both just here together and neither of us want to leave.

My sticky sweet loves, the people I collect in batches like they are cake coming out of the oven, with the two of you in my mind, it never wants to stop smiling. Two parts of me that never wanted to agree seem to open up and stitch themselves together. Independently, you would both be enough: always always always. But conjoined in my heart: I am so swollen, I cannot contain myself.

Acknowledgments

This book could not be what it is without Diana and Kels at Girl Noise Press. Diana — thank you so much for giving my work a home again and including my weird little words in Girl Noise. Kels — thank you for all the work you poured into these words to help them come alive and boogie. To you both — I've separated an artery in my heart just for you both and the Girl Noise we can make!

I want to thank the presses and magazines that gave some of these words a home outside of this book:

- Thank you *JAKE* for giving "Leaky," "I'm Sorry We're Getting Married," and "my sticky sweet(s)" a home.
- Thank you *GMob Magazine* for giving "Wilting" a bog to live in.
- Thank you *Dollar Store Lit Mag* for sharing "I've Fallen in Like" with the world.
- Thank you *ergot* for publishing "The Marriage" alongside collected works not in this manuscript.
- Thank you *Cult Magazine* for sharing "Making the Move."
- Thank you *Tiny Spoon* for allowing "The Blossoming" (a portion of "Waterlog") to emerge within your magazine.
- Thank you to *The Bitchin' Kitsch* for publishing "girl-y" — a true highlight to be a part of your magazine alongside my partner's work.

- Thank you to *The Hooghly Review* for sharing "Best Friends Never Win" with the world.
- Thank you to *Querencia Press* for publishing "Mimed Lives" and "Closet," and for bringing me on board as a reader.
- Thank you *MAYDAY* for giving "you hold me down" a home.
- Thank you *Anti-Heroin Chic* for sharing "Bolides" with everyone.
- Thank you to *So to Speak Journal* for including "you want to feel special" in your summer issue!
- Thank you *cream city review* for including "The Other Man: I Can't Be With" in your Spring 2026 issue.

I also want to thank and hug my family for all of their support throughout my life. Thank you Dad for making us write essays as a punishment when we were younger and for always reading everything I write. Thank you Sister for passing on your love of language — you might be younger, but watching you grow up loving to read made me want to be more like you. Thank you Brother for taking me to all the basement shows and music festivals that helped form me. Thank you to my loving and supportive grandparents — Little Grandma, Grandpa Joe, Nana Susan, Aunt Marie, Gramps.

Thank you to my friends who spent time with these stories in different forms. Thank you Krislyn and Sarah for the weird memes and kind comments on my work. Thank you Hollie for workshopping so much of what went into this book with me. Thank you Kate, Lydia, Sylvia, Jules, Keni, TJ, Libby, TJ, Maddie(s), Gwen, Erin, Kaitlyn, Amber, Kris, Sam, Hazel, and so many more for your love and encouragement.

Thank you endlessly to my partners. H and Z — I don't know if I could have done it without you. You both inspire so many of these stories, even when it may not seem like it, and I am thankful every day that I have you in my life. I love you both more than I could ever put into words (but consider this a good effort at trying to explain).

ABOUT THE AUTHOR

Victoria (Tori) Hood holds an MA in English Literature with a concentration in Creative Writing from the University of Maine where she continues to work as lecturer and mentor. Tori also teaches and tutors at Husson University. She is the winner of FC2's 2021 Ronald Sukenick Innovative Fiction Prize, for her collection of short stories *My Haunted Home* released by FC2. Victoria's poetry chapbook *Death and Darlings* was published in 2022 by Bottlecap Press; her hybrid chapbook *Entries of Boredom and Fear* was published in 2023 by Bottlecap Press. Her book of poetry, *I Am My Mother's Disappointments*, released on Mother's Day from Girl Noise Press (2024). Her work has been published in *Split/Lip Magazine*, *Tiny Spoon*, *Interpret Magazine*, pioneertown, *Querenica Press*, *The Hooghly Review*, *Bitchin' Kitsch*, *ergot.*, *Cult Magazine*, and other various places. Tori now reads for Querenica Press year round and Split/Lip Press for the flash fiction/short story reading period. Overall, she hopes to discomfort, humor and charm.